COOKING
ℱOR THE HEALTH OF IT
Wholesome meal preparations that conform
with U.S.D.A. dietary guidelines.

Gail L. Becker, R.D.

A Benjamin  Company Book

Cover photo: *Blueberry Muffins (page 32), Coq au Vin (page 90), Herb Salad Dressing (page 70), Cranberry Nut Loaf (page 39), Super Chocolate Chip Cookies (page 141), Teriyaki Beef Kabobs (page 76), Corn on the Cob (page 110), Baked Sweet 'N Sour Brussels Sprouts (page 108).*

ABOUT THE AUTHOR

Gail Becker, a registered dietitian, earned her degree in dietetics from Drexel University. She has managed the food and nutrition department of the world's largest weight-control organization, directed dietetics at a large metropolitan hospital, and headed dietetic services for a major food company.

Ms. Becker is a member of the American Dietetics Association, the Society for Nutrition Education, American College of Nutrition, the Institute of Technology, the American Home Economics Association, and many other professional organizations. She conducts nutrition seminars and appears frequently on television and radio programs as an authority on nutrition. Her published articles have appeared in leading women's magazines.

Ms. Becker is the president of a Great Neck, New York based communications company serving the food and nutrition industry.

Recipe Development: Gail Becker Associates, Inc.
Editor: Ellyn Polshek
Project Concept: HBM/Stiefel, Inc.
Photography: Nancy McFarland Studios
Art & Design: Tom Brecklin
Typography: A-Line, Milwaukee

Prepared, Produced, and Published by
           The Benjamin Company, Inc.
           One Westchester Plaza
           Elmsford, New York 10523

ISBN: 0-87502-090-9
Library of Congress Card Catalog Number: 81-67070

Printed in the United States of America
Third Printing: August, 1983

Butter Buds®, Sweet 'N Low®, and Nu-Salt® are registered trademarks of Cumberland Packing Corporation.

Table of Contents

COOKING FOR THE HEALTH OF IT is dedicated to you and the millions of other health and diet-conscious people who want to stay slim and eat healthy but can't because of bland, boring, and tasteless meals. This cookbook changes all that!

Today, more and more Americans realize that too much fat, sugar, and sodium may contribute to many health-related problems, such as dental caries, obesity, heart attacks, and strokes . . . so, they're seeking tasty alternatives.

Butter Buds, Sweet 'N Low, and Nu-Salt are those tasty alternatives. By "switchin' in the kitchen for better nutrition" and using these products in place of butter, margarine, oil, sugar, and salt, the temptation to break your diet and indulge in food that tastes good, but may not be good for you, is eliminated.

These recipes are so tasty, we firmly believe that by preparing them, anyone can keep on a diet and, perhaps for the first time, look forward to both healthful AND delicious meals.

To help keep you slim, healthy, and satisfied at mealtimes, Cumberland Packing corporation will be happy to tell you where you can purchase Butter Buds, Sweet 'N Low, and Nu-Salt in your hometown. Just write to:

Cumberland Packing Corporation
2 Cumberland Street
Brooklyn, New York 11205
Attn: Gail Becker

From Sugar To Sweet 'N Low The History of a Concerned Company

World War II was over. Activities at the great Brooklyn Navy Yard were winding down. The crowds of service men and women who frequented the Cumberland Cafeteria, a popular neighborhood eatery, were thinning out. With the day not far off when there would no longer be a need for the Cumberland Cafeteria, the little restaurant was closed.

In its place, a new and innovative business began — the Cumberland Packing Corporation. Using equipment originally designed to pack tea bags, a process was developed that was destined to revolutionize the sugar industry. With fully-automated and perfected machinery, individual portions of sugar were speedily and economically packaged. Eventually, this led to contracts with major sugar refiners and food distributors.

Despite its small, family-owned origin, Cumberland Packing Corporation of Brooklyn, N.Y., soon grew into a giant in the restaurant service field. People loved the convenience of the separately-wrapped sugar servings that Cumberland made available to restaurants and other large users. Business grew and the company grew along with it.

In the late 50's, Cumberland began its concerned involvement in the country's move toward improved health and dietary habits. Foreseeing the dangers of too much sugar in the diet of most Americans, Cumberland developed a granulated substitute that looked like sugar and tasted like sugar, but which had only a fraction of sugar's caloric content. The only thing needed to make this imaginative new product an immediate hit was a sparkling name.

Cumberland's unique creation was given a name based on the title of a favorite family song. "Sweet and Low," a tune set to a poem by Alfred (Lord) Tennyson, was the inspiration. It became "Sweet 'N Low," and the world's leading granulated sugar substitute had its unforgettable name.

Cumberland continued to package sugar for its restaurant and industrial clientele through the late 1950's and early 1960's, but every year saw increasing popularity of Sweet 'N Low®. By 1963, consumer demand for Sweet 'N Low was so great that

Cumberland heeded the message and began distributing through grocery stores, supermarkets, and drug chains. Popularity increased and it seemed that almost everybody wanted to try the new sweetener.

In 1966, concerned with the distressing connection between the public's excessive use of sugar and the increasing number of overweight Americans, Cumberland made the dramatic decision to put less sugar in American diets, and went out of the sugar business entirely. Instead, the small, vital company dedicated itself totally to improving the health of Americans by creating and marketing only the finest in health and diet products.

While Sweet 'N Low continued to grow in popularity, Americans developed increasing interests in other aspects of their health and diets. Cumberland's active research and development has kept pace with that interest and the changing attitudes of Americans concerned with cholesterol intake, blood pressure levels, and family eating habits in general.

Butter Buds®, 100% Natural Butter-Flavor Granules, grew out of that concern. With practically no cholesterol and only a tiny percentage of the calories found in butter or margarine, Butter Buds provides real butter taste without the fats and calories most of us can do without. Ingeniously versatile and simple to use, Butter Buds is a Cumberland product designed to help consumers control cholesterol intake and calorie consumption without sacrificing good-tasting food.

For those people who must pursue a salt-free or very reduced-sodium diet, Cumberland has been making and selling Nu-Salt® since the mid-1960's. With this remarkable product, anyone can follow a salt-free or reduced-sodium diet while still enjoying the taste of salt. However, as with all salt substitutes, Nu-Salt should not be used without the advice of a physician.

In coming years, the Cumberland Packing Corporation will continue to dedicate itself to the improvement of health and diet worldwide — developing and marketing good-tasting products that are only of the finest quality.

Introduction

It's difficult to pick up a newspaper, magazine, or popular book today that doesn't have something to say about nutrition, health, or fitness. These topics are of significant interest to many of us, and rightly so. Current scientific research in the area of nutrition, health, and fitness provides strong evidence that "we are what we eat."

The Surgeon General's report, *Healthy People,* issued in 1979 points out that chronic degenerative diseases, such as heart disease, hypertension, stroke, diabetes, obesity, and even some forms of cancer, have become major causes of death or disability and are linked to lifestyle factors, including the food we eat. The report proposed modifying the diet of the general public as a means of reducing the incidence of the chronic and degenerative diseases we face.

In February 1980, the U.S. Department of Agriculture and the U.S. Department of Health and Human Services jointly published *Nutrition and Your Health,* Dietary Guidelines for Americans. We feel that the seven recommended guidelines are so basic and important that we have reprinted the entire booklet on pages 9 through 18. We urge you to read them and to refer to them when necessary.

The seven dietary modification recommendations are:

1. Eat a variety of foods
2. Maintain ideal weight
3. Avoid too much fat, saturated fat, and cholesterol
4. Eat foods with adequate starch and fiber
5. Avoid too much sugar
6. Avoid too much sodium
7. If you drink alcohol, do so in moderation

The recommendations are for people who are already generally healthy. Individuals needing special diets to treat a particular disease should consult a physician who may refer them to a dietitian for special instructions.

This book was written especially for you, the normal, reasonably healthy consumer. It introduces you to a delicious new way of cooking that focuses attention on your health and diet. All the recipes have been tested, and the fat, sugar, and salt contents have been reduced to conform to the U.S. Dietary Guideline recommendations.

Developed and taste-tested in our kitchens, these recipes are good for you and easy to make. But they have an even more dominant appeal . . . they taste good! That's because, along with supplying good nutrition, they contain Butter Buds or Sweet 'N Low . . . which go a long way toward providing flavor and zest to the kinds of food you ought to be eating when you're watching your health and diet.

The recipes in this book prove that good, healthy meals don't have to be bland, boring, or tasteless. Using them, you can conform to your modified eating regimen indefinitely, and look forward to every meal!

Each recipe lists the number of calories per serving. We've also listed the carbohydrate, protein, and fat content of each recipe, along with the milligrams of sodium in each serving. What we haven't been able to list is the flavor measure of each recipe. We're confident you will give each recipe a high flavor score.

Dietary Guidelines for Americans

What should you eat to stay healthy?

Hardly a day goes by without someone trying to answer that question. Newspapers, magazines, books, radio, and television give us a lot of advice about what foods we should or should not eat. Unfortunately, much of this advice is confusing.

Some of this confusion exists because we don't know enough about nutrition to identify an "ideal diet" for each individual. People differ — and their food needs vary depending on age, sex, body size, physical activity, and other conditions such as pregnancy or illness.

In those chronic conditions where diet may be important — heart attacks, high blood pressure, strokes, dental caries, diabetes, and some forms of cancer — the roles of specific nutrients have not been defined.

Research does seek to find more precise nutritional requirements and to show better the connections between diet and certain chronic diseases.

But today, what advice should you follow in choosing and preparing the best foods for you and your family?

The following guidelines are suggested for most Americans. They do not apply to people who need special diets because of diseases or conditions that interfere with normal nutrition. These people may require special instruction from trained dietitians, in consultation with their own physicians.

These guidelines are intended for people who are already healthy. No guidelines can guarantee health or well-being. Health depends on many things, including heredity, lifestyle, personality traits, mental health and attitudes, and environment, in addition to diet.

Food alone cannot make you healthy. But good eating habits based on moderation and variety can help keep you healthy and even improve your health.

1. Eat a Variety of Food

You need about 40 different nutrients to stay healthy. These include vitamins and minerals, as well as amino acids (from proteins), essential fatty acids (from vegetable oils and animal fats), and sources of energy (calories from carbohydrates, proteins, and fats). These nutrients are in the foods you normally eat.

Most foods contain more than one nutrient. Milk, for example, provides proteins, fats, sugars, riboflavin and other B-vitamins, vitamin A, calcium, and phosphorus — among other nutrients.

No single food item supplies all the essential nutrients in the amounts that you need. Milk, for instance, contains very little iron or vitamin C. You should, therefore, eat a variety of foods to assure an adequate diet.

The greater the variety, the less likely you are to develop either a deficiency or an excess of any single nutrient. Variety also reduces your likelihood of being exposed to excessive amounts of contaminants in any single food item.

One way to assure variety and, with it, a well-balanced diet is to select foods each day from each of several major groups: for example, fruits and vegetables; cereals, breads, and grains; meats, poultry, eggs, and fish; dry peas and beans, such as soybeans, kidney beans, lima beans, and black-eyed peas, which are good vegetable sources of protein; and milk, cheese, and yogurt.

Fruits and vegetables are excellent sources of vitamins, especially vitamins C and A. Whole grain and enriched breads, cereals, and grain products provide B-vitamins, iron, and energy. Meats supply protein, fat, iron and other minerals, as well as several vitamins, including thiamine and vitamin B_{12}. Dairy products are major sources of calcium and other nutrients.

There are no known advantages to consuming excess amounts of any nutrient. You will rarely need to take vitamin or mineral supplements if you eat a wide variety of foods. There are a few important exceptions to this general statement:

 • **Women in their childbearing years** may need to take iron supplements to replace the iron they lose with menstrual bleeding. Women who are no longer menstruating should not take iron supplements routinely.

• **Women who are pregnant or who are breastfeeding** need more of many nutrients, especially iron, folic acid, vitamin A, calcium, and sources of energy (calories from carbohydrates, proteins, and fats). Detailed advice should come from their physicians or from dieticians.

• **Elderly or very inactive people** may eat relatively little food. Thus, they should pay special attention to avoiding foods that are high in calories but low in other essential nutrients — for example fat, oils, alcohol, and sugars.

Infants also have special nutritional needs. Healthy full-term infants should be breastfed unless there are special problems. The nutrients in human breast milk tend to be digested and absorbed more easily than those in cow's milk. In addition, breast milk may serve to transfer immunity to some diseases from the mother to the infant.

Normally, most babies do not need solid foods until they are 3 to 6 months old. At that time, other foods can be introduced gradually. Prolonged breast or bottle feeding — without solid foods or supplemental iron — can result in iron deficiency.

You should not add salt or sugar to the baby's foods. Infants do not need these "encouragements" — if they are really hungry. The foods themselves contain enough salt and sugar; extra is not necessary.

2. Maintain Ideal Weight

If you are too fat, your chances of developing some chronic disorders are increased. Obesity is associated with high blood pressure, increased levels of blood fats (triglycerides) and cholesterol, and the most common type of diabetes. All of these, in turn, are associated with increased risks of heart attacks and strokes. Thus, you should try to maintain "ideal" weight.

But, how do you determine what the ideal weight is for you?

There is no absolute answer. The table on the following page shows "acceptable" ranges for most adults. If you have been obese since childhood, you may find it difficult to reach or to maintain your weight within the acceptable range. For most people, their weight should not be more than it was when they were young adults (20 or 25 years old).

It is not well understood why some people can eat much more than others and still maintain normal weight. However, one thing is definite: to lose weight, you must take in fewer calories than you burn. This means that you must either select foods containing fewer calories or you must increase your activity — or both.

If you need to lose weight, do so gradually. Steady loss of 1 to 2 pounds a week — until you reach your goal — is relatively safe and more likely to be maintained. Long-term success depends upon acquiring new and better habits of eating and exercise. That is perhaps why "crash" diets usually fail in the long run.

Do not try to lose weight too rapidly. Avoid crash diets that are severely restricted in the variety of foods they allow. Diets containing fewer than 800 calories may be hazardous. Some people have developed kidney stones, disturbing psychological changes, and other complications while following such diets. A few people have died suddenly and without warning.

Suggested Body Weights		
	Range of Acceptable Weight	
Height (feet-inches)	Men (pounds)	Women (pounds)
4'10"		92-119
4'11"		94-122
5'0"		96-125
5'1"		99-128
5'2"	112-141	102-131
5'3"	115-144	105-134
5'4"	118-148	108-138
5'5"	121-152	111-142
5'6"	124-156	114-146
5'7"	128-161	118-150
5'8"	132-166	122-154
5'9"	136-170	126-158
5'10"	140-174	130-163
5'11"	144-179	134-168
6'0"	148-184	138-173
6'1"	152-189	
6'2"	156-194	
6'3"	160-199	
6'4"	164-204	

NOTE: Height with shoes; weight with indoor clothing.

SOURCE: HEW conference on obesity, 1973.

| Approximate Energy Expenditures
(150 Pound Person in Various Activities) ||
Activity	Calories per hour
Lying down or sleeping	80
Sitting	100
Driving an automobile	120
Standing	140
Domestic work	180
Walking, 2½ mph	210
Bicycling, 5½ mph	210
Gardening	220
Golf; lawn mowing, power mower	250
Bowling	270
Walking, 3¾ mph	300
Swimming, ¼ mph	300
Square dancing, volleyball; roller skating	350
Wood chopping or sawing	400
Tennis	420
Skiing, 10 mph	600
Squash and handball	600
Bicycling, 13 mph	660
Running, 10 mph	900

SOURCE: Based on material prepared by Robert E. Johnson, M.D., Ph.D., and colleagues, University of Illinois.

Gradual increase of everyday physical activities like walking or climbing stairs can be very helpful. The chart below gives the calories used per hour in different activities.

A pound of body fat contains 3500 calories. To lose 1 pound of fat, you will need to burn 3500 calories more than you consume. If you burn 500 calories more a day than you consume, you will lose 1 pound of fat a week. Thus, if you normally burn 1700 calories a day, you theoretically expect to lose a pound of fat each week if you adhere to a 1200-calorie-per-day diet.

Do not attempt to reduce your weight below the acceptable range. Severe weight loss may be associated with nutrient deficiencies, menstrual irregularities, infertility, hair loss, skin changes, cold intolerance, severe constipation, psychiatric disturbances, and other complications.

If you lose weight suddenly or for unknown reasons, see a physician. Unexplained weight loss may be an early clue to an unsuspected underlying disorder.

To Lose Weight
- Increase physical activity
- Eat less fat and fatty foods
- Eat less sugar and sweets
- Avoid too much alcohol

To Improve Eating Habits
- Eat slowly
- Prepare smaller portions
- Avoid "seconds"

3. Avoid Too Much Fat, Saturated Fat, and Cholesterol

If you have high blood cholesterol level, you have a greater chance of having a heart attack. Other factors can also increase your risk of heart attack — high blood pressure and cigarette smoking, for example — but high blood cholesterol is clearly a major dietary risk indicator.

Populations like ours with diets high in saturated fats and cholesterol tend to have high blood cholesterol levels. Individuals within these populations usually have greater risks of having heart attacks than people eating low-fat, low-cholesterol diets.

Eating extra saturated fat and cholesterol will increase blood cholesterol levels in most people. However, there are wide variations among people — related to heredity and the way each person's body uses cholesterol.

Some people can consume diets high in saturated fats and cholesterol and still keep normal blood cholesterol levels. Other people, unfortunately, have high blood cholesterol levels even if they eat low-fat, low-cholesterol diets.

There is controversy about what recommendations are appropriate for healthy Americans. But for the U.S. population *as a whole*, reduction in our current intake of total fat, saturated fat, and cholesterol is sensible. This suggestion is especially appropriate for people who have high blood pressure or who smoke.

The recommendations are not meant to prohibit the use of any specific food item or to prevent you from eating a variety of foods. For example, eggs and organ meats (such as liver) contain cholesterol, but they also contain many essential vitamins and minerals, as well as protein. Such items can be eaten in moderation, as long as your overall cholesterol intake is not excessive. If you prefer whole milk to skim milk, you can reduce your intake of fats from foods other than milk.

To Avoid too much Fat, Saturated Fat, and Cholesterol

- Choose lean meat, fish, poultry, dry beans and peas as your protein sources
- Moderate your use of eggs and organ meats (such as liver)
- Limit your intake of butter, cream hydrogenated margarines, shortenings and coconut oil, and foods made from such products
- Trim excess fat off meats
- Broil, bake, or boil rather than fry
- Read labels carefully to determine both amount and types of fat contained in foods

4. Eat Foods with Adequate Starch and Fiber

The major sources of energy in the average U.S. diet are carbohydrates and fats. (Proteins and alcohol also supply energy, but to a lesser extent.) If you limit your fat intake, you should increase your calories from carbohydrates to supply your body's energy needs.

In trying to reduce your weight to "ideal" levels, carbohydrates have an advantage over fats: carbohydrates contain less than half the number of calories per ounce than fats.

Complex carbohydrate foods are better than *simple* carbohydrates in this regard. Simple carbohydrates — such as sugars — provide calories but little else in the way of nutrients. Complex carbohydrate foods — such as beans, peas, nuts, seeds, fruits and vegetables, and whole grain breads, cereals, and products — contain many essential nutrients in addition to calories.

Increasing your consumption of certain complex carbohydrates can also help increase dietary fiber. The average American diet is relatively low in fiber. Eating more foods high in fiber tends to reduce the symptoms of chronic constipation, diverticulosis, and some types of "irritable bowel." There is also concern that low fiber diets might increase the risk of developing cancer of the colon, but whether this is true is not yet known.

To make sure you get enough fiber in your diet, you should eat fruits and vegetables, whole grain breads and cereals. There is no reason to add fiber to foods that do not already contain it.

5. Avoid Too Much Sugar

The major health hazard from eating too much sugar is tooth decay (dental caries). The risk of caries is not simply a matter of how much sugar you eat. The risk increases the more frequently you eat sugar and sweets, especially if you eat between meals, and if you eat foods that stick to the teeth. For example, frequent snacks of sticky candy, or dates, or daylong use of soft drinks may be more harmful than adding sugar to your morning cup of coffee — at least as far as your teeth are concerned.

Obviously, there is more to healthy teeth than avoiding sugars. Careful dental hygiene and exposure to adequate amounts of fluoride in the water are especially important.

Contrary to widespread opinion, too much sugar in your diet does not seem to cause diabetes. The most common type of diabetes is seen in obese adults, and avoiding sugar, without correcting the overweight, will not solve the problem. There is also no convincing evidence that sugar causes heart attacks or blood vessel diseases.

Estimates indicate that Americans use on the average more than 130 pounds of sugars and sweeteners a year. This means the risk of tooth decay is increased not only by the sugar in the sugar bowl but by the sugars and syrups in jams, jellies, candies, cookies, soft drinks, cakes, and pies, as well as sugars found in products such as breakfast cereals, catsup, flavored milks, and ice cream. Frequently, the ingredient label will provide a clue to the amount of sugars in a product.

To Avoid Excessive Sugars

- Use less of all sugars, including white sugar, brown sugar, raw sugar, honey, and syrups
- Eat less of foods containing these sugars, such as candy, soft drinks, ice cream, cakes, cookies
- Select fresh fruits or fruits canned without sugar, or light syrup rather than heavy syrup
- Read food labels for clues on sugar content — if the names sucrose, glucose, maltose, dextrose, lactose, fructose, or syrups appear first, then there is a large amount of sugar
- Remember, how often you eat sugar is as important as how much sugar you eat

6. Avoid too Much Sodium

Table salt contains sodium and chloride — both are essential elements. Sodium is also present in many beverages and foods that we eat, especially in certain processed foods, condiments, sauces, pickled foods, salty snacks, and sandwich meats. Baking soda, baking powder, monosodium glutamate (MSG), soft drinks, and even many medications (many antacids, for instance) contain sodium.

It is not surprising that adults in the United States take in much more sodium than they need.

The major hazard of excessive sodium is for persons who have high blood pressure. Not everyone is equally susceptible. In the United States, approximately 17 percent of adults have high blood pressure. Sodium intake is but one of the factors known to affect blood pressure. Obesity, in particular, seems to play a major role.

In populations with low-sodium intakes, high blood pressure is rare. In contrast, in populations with high-sodium intakes, high blood pressure is common. If people with high blood pressure severely restrict their sodium intakes, their blood pressures will *usually* fall — although not always to normal levels.

At present, there is no good way to predict who will develop high blood pressure, though certain groups, such as blacks, have a higher incidence. Low-sodium diets might help some of these people avoid high blood pressure if they could be identified before they develop the condition.

Since most Americans eat more sodium than is needed, consider reducing your sodium intake. Use less table salt. Eat sparingly those foods to which large amounts of sodium have been added. Remember that up to half of sodium intake may be "hidden," either as part of the naturally occurring food or, more often, as part of a preservative or flavoring agent that has been added.

To Avoid Too Much Sodium

- Learn to enjoy the unsalted flavors of foods
- Cook with only small amounts of added salt
- Add little or no salt to food at the table
- Limit your intake of salty foods, such as potato chips, pretzels, salted nuts and popcorn, condiments (soy sauce, steak sauce, garlic salt), cheese, pickled foods, cured meats

- Read food labels carefully to determine the amounts of sodium in processed foods and snack items

7. If You Drink Alcohol, Do So In Moderation

Alcoholic beverages tend to be high in calories and low in other nutrients. Even moderate drinkers may need to drink less if they wish to achieve ideal weight.

On the other hand, heavy drinkers may lose their appetites for foods containing essential nutrients. Vitamin and mineral deficiencies occur commonly in heavy drinkers — in part, because of poor intake, but also because alcohol alters the absorption and use of some essential nutrients.

Sustained or excessive alcohol consumption by pregnant women has caused birth defects. Pregnant women should limit alcohol intake to 2 ounces or less on any single day.

Heavy drinking may also cause a variety of serious conditions, such as cirrhosis of the liver and some neurological disorders. Cancer of the throat and neck is much more common in people who drink and smoke than in people who don't.

One or two drinks daily appear to cause no harm in adults. If you drink you should do so in moderation.

The section "Dietary Guidelines for Americans" was reprinted from NUTRITION AND YOUR HEALTH from the U.S. Department of Agriculture and the U.S. Department of Health, Education and Welfare.

BUTTER BUDS®

Butter Flavor without the Calories or Cholesterol

If you love the flavor of butter, but want to cut your calorie or cholesterol intake, use Butter Buds instead of butter, margarine, or oil. Although margarine and vegetable oil are cholesterol-free, they are not low in calories. A tablespoon of either butter or margarine contains approximately 100 calories, and vegetable oil has about 120 calories per tablespoon. There are about 50 calories in a tablespoon of diet margarine, but a tablespoon equivalent of Butter Buds contains only 6 calories.

Butter Buds contains 99% less cholesterol than butter. Most medical opinion today holds that excessive cholesterol intake can be a factor in heart disease, hypertension, atherosclerosis, and stroke. The cholesterol we eat tends to collect in our arteries, thereby reducing the opening and causing excessive pressure to build up in the arteries. By reducing the amount of cholesterol we eat, we can help prevent the high cholesterol level that doctors warn us about.

Butter Buds also contains about 25% less sodium than salted butter or margarine. A tablespoon of liquid Butter Buds contains 110 milligrams sodium, whereas the same amount of butter or margarine contains 138 milligrams sodium.

Butter Buds are 100% natural butter flavor granules. They are sold in boxes of eight packets. Each packet is equal in butter-flavor to a quarter pound (one stick) of butter or margarine. In liquid form, one packet of Butter Buds can be substituted in cooking for a half-cup of melted butter, margarine, or vegetable oil.

Butter Buds can be sprinkled dry from the packet over Popcorn (page 143) or as a topping for Baked Chicken (page 84). They can be made into a liquid by mixing the contents of one packet with one half cup (4 ounces) of hot tap water. In liquid form, Butter Buds are quite versatile. For a taste treat, the mixture can be brushed over corn on the cob or on a toasted English Muffin. Use it instead of melted butter, margarine, or vegetable oil in your favorite recipes. In this book, we've used Butter Buds in appetizers, beverages, soups, salad dressings, sauces, main dishes, vegetables, and for quick breads and desserts.

Because Butter Buds is virtually fat-free, we do not recommend that you use it for frying. (If you're watching your calories, you've probably been advised not to fry foods anyway, so this is no hardship.) If you do want to fry things, try using a non-stick skillet, or a non-stick coating agent, and flavor your foods with Butter Buds. You'll find it a joy.

Butter Buds can be conveniently stored on your kitchen shelf with your seasonings and spices, since it needs no refrigeration until reconstituted. And, because in dry form, Butter Buds is foil-packed, it goes anywhere you do, camping, fishing, picnicking, even to restaurants! When made liquid, it stays fresh up to three days in your refrigerator.

In this book, the modified- and reduced-fat recipes using Butter Buds are denoted by the 🍞 symbol. You can reduce the fat content of the other recipes in this book by substituting Butter Buds for margarine or vegetable oil. The substitution for diet margarine is half as much as for regular margarine.

BUTTER BUDS CONVERSION CHART

How to reconstitute Butter Buds:

Mix one packet (8 level tsps.) with 1/2 cup (4 oz.) of hot tap water. Shake well to make 4 oz. of delicious melted butter flavor. Pour over or stir into any food you cook.

Liquid Butter Buds	Butter/Margarine	Vegetable Oil
1/2 cup (1 packet) equals	8 tablespoons 1 stick 1/2 cup 1/4 lb. 4 ounces	1/2 cup
1/4 cup equals	4 tablespoons 1/2 stick 1/4 cup 1/8 lb. 2 ounces	1/4 cup
2 tablespoons equal	2 tablespoons	2 tablespoons
2 teaspoons equal	2 teaspoons	2 teaspoons

SWEET 'N LOW®
Sugar Sweetness without the Calories

If you're one of those people for whom a meal isn't complete without something sweet, but you want to cut down the amount of sugar you consume, this book features many delicious recipes which use Sweet 'N Low. Not only can you trim calories from your diet by using Sweet 'N Low as a substitute for sugar, but you will also reduce the risk of dental caries (cavities). Eating too much sugar is often linked with excess weight and most reducing diets recommend that sugar intake be cut.

Sweet 'N Low is available boxed in bulk form or individual packets. Each familiar pink packet has the sweetening power of two teaspoons of sugar but contains only about 4 calories. There are about 30 calories in two teaspoons of sugar. For convenience and consistency, we've specified individual packets of Sweet 'N Low in this collection of recipes. If you have the bulk package, use two of the supplied measuring spoonfuls of Sweet 'N Low for each packet called for.

The reduced sugar recipes in this cookbook using Sweet 'N Low are denoted by the ⑤ symbol. You can reduce the sugar content of other recipes in this book and of your own favorites at home by using this simple conversion table:

FOR Granulated Sugar		USE Sweet 'N Low
1/4 cup	=	3 packets or 1 teaspoon
1/3 cup	=	4 packets or 1 1/3 teaspoons
1/2 cup	=	6 packets or 2 teaspoons
1 cup	=	12 packets or 4 teaspoons

NU-SALT®
Salt Taste Without Added Sodium

If your doctor has recommended a reduced sodium diet, but your meals seem bland and tasteless, Nu-Salt may be for you. It gives the zesty taste of salt without adding sodium.

Sodium is a mineral found in nature and in most foods. A good deal of the sodium we consume comes from table salt (sodium chloride) which we use in cooking or at the table. But a lot also comes from food that doesn't necessarily taste "salty." Sodium is an important nutrient, but most Americans tend to consume much more than is necessary.

The connection between excessive sodium intake and hypertension (high blood pressure) has long been recognized. Many people have elevated blood pressure but are not aware of it. Yet high blood pressure significantly increases the risk of heart attack, stroke, or kidney failure. Controlling high blood pressure is one of the most common reasons a doctor may recommend reducing the amount of salt or sodium in the diet.

A first step in reducing the amount of sodium in your diet could be to remove the salt shaker from the table and replace it with a blend of your favorite salt-free spices and herbs. If advised by your doctor, you can use Nu-Salt salt substitute for added zest and appeal. Nu-Salt looks like salt, sprinkles like salt, and tastes like salt. But it is completely sodium-free.

Nu-Salt is available in 3-ounce table shakers and in boxes of individual packets.The reduced sodium recipes in this book are denoted by a ⬤ symbol. With your doctor's permission you can use Nu-Salt for seasoning any of them. The sodium content is shown for all the recipes, so you can plan healthful sodium-controlled meals.

NUTRITIONAL INFORMATION

	Serving Size (Approximate)	Approx. Sodium (mg)	Approx. Calories	Approx. Cholesterol (mg)
NU-SALT	1/8 tsp. (1 packet)	Trace*	0	0
Salt	1 tsp.	2132	0	0
SWEET 'N LOW	3/8 tsp. (1 packet)	3.6	4	0
Sugar	1 tsp.	Trace*	15	0
BUTTER BUDS (dry)	1 tsp.	110	6	.4
BUTTER BUDS (liquid)	1 tbsp.	110	6	.4
Butter	1 tbsp.	138	100	36.0
Margarine	1 tbsp.	138	100	0

*Trace: Present in insignificant amounts. Less than 1 mg.

Breakfast and Brunches

Whether it's a weekday breakfast or weekend brunch, these are very important meals to start your day off right nutritionally. They don't have to be high in salt, cholesterol, or calories either, if you serve Asparagus Cheese Crêpes (page 26) or delicious homemade Low-Salt Pork Sausage Patties (page 29). Butter Buds granules blend well in scrambled eggs, too, adding rich butter flavor without lots of extra calories. In a hurry? Try Trim Slim Cinnamon Toast (page 24) or the marvelously rich and creamy, but surprisingly low in calories, Buttered Almond Breakfast Shake (page 43).

Trim Slim Cinnamon Toast

 2 servings

2 teaspoons sugar
Cinnamon as desired
1/4 cup liquid Butter Buds

2 slices enriched white
toast

In small dish, combine sugar and cinnamon. Using pastry brush, generously brush Butter Buds on toast. Sprinkle with cinnamon mixture.

PER SERVING (1 slice):	Calories: 95	Protein: 2gm
Carbohydrate: 17gm	Fat: 1gm	Sodium: 334mg

By using Butter Buds instead of butter in this recipe, you have saved 65 calories and 22 mg cholesterol per serving. To save an additional 15 calories per serving, substitute 1 packet Sweet 'N Low for the sugar in this recipe. You'll also be saving 4 grams carbohydrate.

Cheese Toast Roll-Ups

 6 servings

3/4 cup (about 6 ounces) dry-
curd cottage cheese
1/2 cup (about 2 ounces) grated
sharp cheddar cheese
1 packet Butter Buds
1 packet Butter Buds, made
into liquid
2 tablespoons chopped pimiento
1 tablespoon chopped fresh
parsley

1/2 teaspoon dry mustard
1/4 teaspoon basil
1/4 teaspoon marjoram
1/4 teaspoon oregano
Freshly ground pepper
to taste
Dash nutmeg
12 slices enriched white
bread

Preheat oven to 400°F. Blend cheeses with 1 packet dry Butter Buds. (For best results, use potato masher to soften cheese before blending with other ingredients.) Add 3 tablespoons liquid Butter Buds, pimiento, parsley, mustard, basil, marjoram, oregano, pepper, and nutmeg. Blend thoroughly. Trim off bread crusts. Use rolling pin to flatten bread slices. Spread each slice of bread with slightly rounded tablespoon of cheese mixture. Gently roll up each slice and place seam down on non-stick baking sheet. Bake until outside surface is lightly browned, 5 to 7 minutes. Remove from oven and brush generously with remaining liquid Butter Buds. Return to oven until cheese melts and outside surface is golden brown, about 5 minutes.

PER SERVING (2 roll-ups):	Calories: 210	Protein: 17gm
Carbohydrate: 25gm	Fat: 5gm	Sodium: 725mg

By using Butter Buds instead of butter in this recipe, you have saved 250 calories and 93 mg cholesterol per serving.

Banana Toast

 4 servings

1 packet Butter Buds, mixed with 1/4 cup hot water
1 tablespoon honey
1/4 teaspoon cinnamon

4 slices enriched white toast
2 medium-size bananas, thinly sliced

Preheat broiler. In covered jar, combine Butter Buds, honey, and cinnamon; shake well. With pastry brush, spread sauce on each slice of toast. Arrange banana slices on toast, covering entire surface. Brush with additional sauce. Broil 2 to 3 minutes, or until bananas begin to bubble.

PER SERVING (1 slice):	Calories: 155	Protein: 3gm
Carbohydrate: 34gm	Fat: 1gm	Sodium: 270mg

By using Butter Buds instead of butter in this recipe, you have saved 188 calories and 70 mg cholesterol per serving.

Sesame Toast

 12 servings

3 tablespoons sesame seeds
1/3 cup liquid Butter Buds
1 teaspoon parsley flakes

1 loaf (about 12 inches long) Italian or French bread

Preheat oven to 400°F. Spread sesame seeds in baking pan and brown lightly in oven. Reduce oven to 350°F. Combine seeds with Butter Buds and parsley. Cut bread into 1-inch-thick slices. With pastry brush, spread each slice on both sides with sauce. Wrap bread in foil. Heat about 15 to 20 minutes.

PER SERVING (1 slice):	Calories: 120	Protein: 4gm
Carbohydrate: 22gm	Fat: 1gm	Sodium: 270mg

By using Butter Buds instead of butter in this recipe, you have saved 45 calories and 18 mg cholesterol per serving.

Asparagus Cheese Crêpes ⒷⒷ 4 servings

1 package (10 ounces) frozen
   cut asparagus
1 cup low-fat cottage cheese
2 tablespoons low-fat milk
1 tablespoon fresh lemon juice
1 1/2 teaspoons minced onion flakes

8 Low-Calorie Crêpes
   (below)
Herb Butter Sauce
   (page 30)

Preheat oven to 350°F. Cook asparagus according to package directions; drain well. Chop into small pieces; place in medium-size bowl. In blender container, combine cottage cheese, milk, lemon juice, and onion flakes. Cover and process at medium speed 20 to 30 seconds. Fold cottage cheese mixture into chopped asparagus. Fill crêpes with 2 rounded tablespoons of cheese mixture. Fold over and place in non-stick baking dish. Bake, covered, 15 to 20 minutes, or until heated throughout. Before serving, spoon about 1 tablespoon Herb Butter Sauce over each crêpe.

PER SERVING (2 crêpes):	Calories: 210	Protein: 17gm
Carbohydrate: 27gm	Fat: 4gm	Sodium: 665mg

Note: If you don't own a non-stick baking dish, you can spray your baking dish with a non-stick coating agent.

Low-Calorie Crêpes ⒷⒷ 12 crêpes

1 cup all-purpose flour
1 1/4 cups low-fat milk
1 packet Butter Buds

3 eggs
1/8 teaspoon salt

Mixer or whisk method: In medium bowl, combine all ingredients. Beat with electric mixer or whisk until smooth.

Blender method: Combine ingredients in blender container. Cover and process at medium speed about 1 minute. Scrape down sides with rubber spatula and blend for another 15 seconds, or until smooth.

Refrigerate 1 hour or more. If batter separates, stir gently before cooking. Cook on upside-down crêpe griddle or in traditional pan.

PER SERVING (1 crêpe):	Calories: 60	Protein: 3gm
Carbohydrate: 9gm	Fat: 1gm	Sodium: 70mg

By using Butter Buds instead of butter in this recipe, you have saved 63 calories and 23 mg cholesterol per serving.

Asparagus Cheese Crêpes, Poached Pears with
Blueberry Sauce (page 150),
Broccoli Cheese Pie (page 28).

Broccoli Cheese Pie

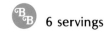 6 servings

1 package (10 ounces) frozen chopped broccoli
1/3 cup chopped onion
1 tablespoon lemon juice
1/2 teaspoon nutmeg
1/8 teaspoon freshly ground pepper

1 9-inch Low-Sodium Pie Crust (page 134)
1/3 cup grated Parmesan cheese
4 eggs
1/2 cup low-fat milk
1/4 cup liquid Butter Buds

Preheat oven to 425°F. Cook broccoli according to package directions; drain well. While broccoli is draining, combine onion, lemon juice, nutmeg, and pepper in medium-size bowl. Add broccoli and mix well. Pour into pie shell and sprinkle with Parmesan cheese. Mix eggs with milk and Butter Buds. Pour over broccoli mixture. Place filled pie pan on cookie sheet and bake 10 minutes. Reduce heat to 350°F and bake about 30 minutes, or until filling is set.

PER SERVING (1/6 pie):	Calories: 230	Protein: 11gm
Carbohydrate: 21gm	Fat: 11gm	Sodium: 320mg

By using Butter Buds instead of butter in this recipe, you have saved 63 calories and 23 mg cholesterol per serving.

Easy Sticky Buns

 8 servings

1 packet Butter Buds, made into liquid
1/4 cup chopped nuts
1/4 cup flaked coconut
3 tablespoons firmly packed light brown sugar

1 teaspoon cinnamon
1 package (10 1/2 ounces) refrigerated biscuits

Preheat oven to 350°F. In round cake pan or baking dish, combine all ingredients except biscuits. Separate biscuits and roll in syrup mixture to coat. Arrange in single layer on top of syrup. Bake 15 to 20 minutes, or until buns are well browned. While still warm, invert on serving plate.

PER SERVING (1 bun):	Calories: 145	Protein: 4gm
Carbohydrate: 23gm	Fat: 4gm	Sodium: 420mg

By using Butter Buds instead of butter in this recipe, you have saved 94 calories and 35 mg cholesterol per serving.

Noodle Pudding

 4 servings

2 ounces uncooked enriched
   noodles
2 eggs
1 cup evaporated skim milk,
   undiluted
1/2 cup part skim ricotta
   cheese

3 packets Sweet 'N Low
1 teaspoon vanilla
1 teaspoon grated lemon
   peel
1 medium-size apple,
   peeled and grated
1/4 cup raisins

Preheat oven to 350°F. Cook noodles according to package directions, omitting salt. With electric mixer, beat eggs in large bowl. Add milk, ricotta cheese, Sweet 'N Low, vanilla, and lemon peel. Beat until smooth. Stir in noodles, apple, and raisins. Turn into 1-quart casserole. Bake 1 hour, or until knife inserted in center comes out clean.

PER SERVING (1/2 cup):	Calories: 235	Protein: 14gm
Carbohydrate: 31gm	Fat: 6gm	Sodium: 145mg

Low-Salt Pork Sausage Patties

N·S 9 servings

1 pound lean ground pork
1 packet Butter Buds, mixed
   with 1/4 cup hot water
1/2 teaspoon basil
1/2 teaspoon thyme
1/2 teaspoon sage
1/4 teaspoon cumin
1/4 teaspoon marjoram

1/4 teaspoon freshly
   ground pepper
1/4 teaspoon oregano
1/4 teaspoon cayenne
1/8 teaspoon garlic powder
1/8 teaspoon nutmeg
1/8 teaspoon ginger
1 tablespoon fresh bread
   crumbs

Crumble pork in large bowl. In separate bowl, mix remaining ingredients; add pork and mix well. Refrigerate seasoned pork in covered bowl, about 6 hours or overnight. Preheat oven to 400°F. Form pork mixture into nine patties. Bake on rack in shallow pan 20 to 25 minutes.

PER SERVING (1½-ounce patty):	Calories: 100	Protein: 11gm
Carbohydrate: 2gm	Fat: 5gm	Sodium: 125mg

By using Butter Buds instead of butter in this recipe, you have saved 84 calories and 31 mg cholesterol per serving.

Special Brunch Stacks

 4 servings

1 package (10 ounces) frozen
    asparagus spears
1 packet Butter Buds
2 tablespoons all-purpose
    flour
1 cup low-fat milk
1/4 teaspoon dry mustard
    Dash cayenne

1/4 teaspoon Worcestershire
    sauce
1/2 cup grated Cheddar
    cheese
4 English muffins, split
    and toasted
1/2 pound sliced cooked
    turkey
    Paprika

Cook asparagus according to package directions. Drain and set aside. In small saucepan, combine Butter Buds, flour, and milk; mix well. Season with mustard, cayenne, and Worcestershire. Heat, stirring constantly, until slightly thickened. Add cheese and stir until melted. Arrange 2 muffin halves on each serving plate. Place 1 ounce turkey and 2 or 3 asparagus spears on each muffin. Pour about 2 tablespoons cheese sauce over top and sprinkle with paprika.

PER SERVING (2 muffin halves): Calories: 370	Protein: 31gm
Carbohydrate: 40gm Fat: 10gm	Sodium: 625mg

By using Butter Buds instead of butter in this recipe, you have saved 188 calories and 70 mg cholesterol per serving.

Herb Butter Sauce

 1/2 cup sauce

1 packet Butter Buds, made
    into liquid
2 tablespoons lemon juice
1 teaspoon parsley flakes

1 teaspoon dehydrated
    chives
1/2 teaspoon tarragon
1/8 teaspoon onion powder

Combine all ingredients in small saucepan and heat just until hot, mixing well. Spoon sauce over your favorite vegetable or meat crêpe.

PER SERVING (1 tablespoon): Calories: 5	Protein: trace
Carbohydrate: 1gm Fat: trace	Sodium: 110mg

By using Butter Buds instead of butter in this recipe, you have saved 188 calories and 70 mg cholesterol per serving.

Eggs Benedict

 2 servings

4 eggs
4 slices (4 ounces) cooked turkey
    breast
2 English muffins, split and
    toasted

1/2 cup Mock Hollandaise
    (below)
1 tablespoon chopped
    fresh parsley

Poach eggs. Place 1 slice turkey on each muffin half and top with 1 egg. Spoon 2 tablespoons Mock Hollandaise over each egg. Garnish with parsley.

PER SERVING (2 muffin halves): Calories: 455		Protein: 36gm
Carbohydrate: 31gm	Fat: 21gm	Sodium: 550mg

Nice to know: By using only the whites of the eggs, you will save 115 calories, 5 gm protein, 10 gm fat, and 25 mg sodium per serving. If you use an amount of egg substitute equivalent to 4 eggs, you will save 65 calories and 10 gm fat per serving. However, you will be adding 3 gm protein, 5 gm carbohydrate, and 150 mg sodium per serving.

Mock Hollandaise

 About 1 cup

1 cup Butter Buds "Mayo"
    (page 65)

1/4 cup hot water
2 teaspoons lemon juice

Combine all ingredients and mix well. Serve warm over broccoli, asparagus, or Eggs Benedict.

PER SERVING (2 tablespoons): Calories: 75		Protein: 1gm
Carbohydrate: 2gm	Fat: 7gm	Sodium: 195mg

By using Butter Buds instead of vegetable oil in this recipe, you have saved 114 calories per serving.

Cinnamon Raisin Biscuits

 1 dozen biscuits

1 cup sifted all-purpose flour
1 cup whole-wheat flour
1 tablespoon baking powder
1 teaspoon cinnamon
3 packets Sweet 'N Low

1/4 teaspoon salt
1/4 cup (1/2 stick) margarine
1/2 cup raisins
3/4 cup low-fat milk

Preheat oven to 425°F. In medium-size bowl, sift together dry ingredients. With pastry blender or knife, cut in margarine until mixture resembles coarse oatmeal. Add raisins and stir to mix. Make a well in center of flour mixture. Pour in milk. Stir rapidly with spatula until dough is just moist enough to leave sides of bowl to form a ball. Knead dough lightly 10 to 15 times, then roll or pat out on floured surface to 1/2-inch thickness. Cut into circles with biscuit cutter. Fit close together on non-stick baking sheet. Bake 10 to 15 minutes, or until golden brown. Transfer to cooling racks.

PER SERVING (1 biscuit):	Calories: 106	Protein: 3gm
Carbohydrate: 18gm	Fat: 3gm	Sodium: 152mg

Note: If you don't own a non-stick baking sheet, you can spray your baking sheet with a non-stick coating agent.

Blueberry Muffins

 1 dozen muffins

1 1/2 cups all-purpose flour
1/2 cup sugar
2 teaspoons baking powder
1/2 teaspoon salt

1 egg
1/2 cup low-fat milk
1/4 cup liquid Butter Buds
1 1/2 cups blueberries

Preheat oven to 400°F. In large bowl, combine dry ingredients. Add egg, milk, and Butter Buds. Stir just until batter is moistened. Rinse and drain blueberries and dust with additional flour. Add to batter; lightly stir to combine. Spray muffin tins with non-stick coating agent. Drop 2 tablespoons batter in each muffin cup. Bake 20 to 25 minutes, or until golden brown.

PER SERVING (1 muffin):	Calories: 115	Protein: 3gm
Carbohydrate: 25gm	Fat: 1gm	Sodium: 155mg

By using Butter Buds instead of butter in this recipe, you have saved 27 calories and 12 mg cholesterol per serving.

Bran Muffins 2 dozen muffins

4 cups raisin bran cereal
2 1/2 cups all-purpose flour
1 1/2 cups sugar
2 1/2 teaspoons baking soda
1 teaspoon salt

2 eggs
2 cups buttermilk
1 packet Butter Buds,
   made into liquid

Preheat oven to 400°F. In large bowl, mix cereal, flour, sugar, baking soda, and salt. Add eggs, buttermilk, and Butter Buds and mix well. Spray muffin tins with non-stick coating agent. Fill muffin cups two-thirds full and bake 15 to 20 minutes.

PER SERVING (1 muffin):	Calories: 120	Protein: 3gm
Carbohydrate: 27gm	Fat: 1gm	Sodium: 277mg

By using Butter Buds instead of butter in this recipe, you have saved 31 calories and 12 mg cholesterol per serving.

Baked Carrot Squares 16 servings

1 cup sifted all-purpose flour
1 teaspoon baking powder
1/4 teaspoon cinnamon
1/8 teaspoon nutmeg
1/8 teaspoon salt
6 packets Sweet 'N Low

1/2 teaspoon baking soda
1 packet Butter Buds,
   made into liquid
1 egg, beaten
1 cup grated carrots
1 cup raisins

Preheat oven to 350°F. Spray 8-inch square baking pan with non-stick coating agent. In medium-size bowl, combine flour, baking powder, cinnamon, nutmeg, salt, and Sweet 'N Low. In separate bowl, dissolve baking soda in Butter Buds; add to dry ingredients. Stir in egg. Add carrots and raisins and mix thoroughly. Pour into prepared pan. Bake 30 minutes, or until toothpick inserted in center comes out clean. Cool and cut into 2-inch squares.

PER SERVING (one 2-inch square):	Calories: 60	Protein: 1gm
Carbohydrate: 14gm	Fat: trace	Sodium: 80mg

By using Butter Buds instead of butter in this recipe, you have saved 47 calories and 18 mg cholesterol per serving.

Note: There's no need to spray with a non-stick coating agent if you own a non-stick 8-inch square baking pan.

Orange Muffins 1 dozen muffins

2 cups sifted all-purpose flour
6 packets Sweet 'N Low
1 tablespoon baking powder
1/2 teaspoon salt
1 egg, beaten

1 cup low-fat milk
2 tablespoons margarine, melted
2 teaspoons finely grated orange rind

Preheat oven to 425°F. Spray muffin tin with non-stick coating agent. Sift dry ingredients into medium-size bowl. In separate bowl, combine egg with milk, margarine, and orange rind. Beat with fork or whisk to mix thoroughly. Make a well in center of dry ingredients. Pour in liquid ingredients; stir quickly until dry ingredients are just moistened and mixture is still slightly lumpy. Divide batter into muffin cups, filling each two-thirds full. Bake 15 to 20 minutes, or until golden brown and toothpick inserted in center comes out clean. Loosen edges of muffins. Let stand 1 or 2 minutes. Turn onto cooling racks.

PER SERVING (1 muffin):	Calories: 100	Protein: 3gm
Carbohydrate: 16gm	Fat: 3gm	Sodium: 200mg

By substituting 2 tablespoons liquid Butter Buds for the margarine in this recipe, you can save 15 calories, 1 gm fat, 6 mg cholesterol, and 5 mg sodium per muffin.

Note: There's no need to spray with a non-stick coating agent if you own a non-stick muffin tin.

Banana Bran Muffins 1 dozen muffins

1 cup sifted all-purpose flour
6 packets Sweet 'N Low
1 teaspoon baking powder
1 1/2 cups bran cereal
1 teaspoon baking soda
3/4 cup low-fat milk

2 tablespoons margarine, melted
4 teaspoons honey
2 teaspoons molasses
1/2 cup mashed banana
1 egg, beaten

Preheat oven to 425°F. Spray muffin tins with non-stick coating agent. In medium-size bowl, sift together flour, Sweet 'N Low, and baking powder; stir in bran. In separate bowl, dissolve baking soda in milk. Blend margarine, honey, molasses, banana, and egg. Combine with milk. Beat with fork or whisk to mix thoroughly. Make well in center of dry ingredients. Pour in liquid ingredients; stir quickly until dry ingredients are just moistened and mixture is still slightly lumpy. Divide batter into muffin cups, filling each two-thirds full. Bake 15 to 20 minutes, or until toothpick inserted in center comes out clean. Loosen edges of muffins. Let stand 1 or 2 minutes. Turn onto cooling racks.

PER SERVING (1 muffin):	Calories: 100	Protein: 3gm
Carbohydrate: 18gm	Fat: 2gm	Sodium: 180mg

By substituting 2 tablespoons liquid Butter Buds for the margarine in this recipe, you can save 15 calories, 2 gm fat, 6 mg cholesterol, and 5 mg of sodium per muffin.

Note: There's no need to spray with a non-stick coating agent if you own a non-stick muffin tin.

Raised Biscuits About 2 1/2 dozen biscuits

2 packets active dry yeast
3/4 cup lukewarm water
4 cups sifted all-purpose
    flour
1 tablespoon sugar

2 packets Butter Buds
1/3 cup vegetable oil
1/4 cup water
1 packet Butter Buds,
    made into liquid

Soften yeast in water. Let stand 5 minutes. In large bowl, sift together flour, sugar, and 2 packets dry Butter Buds. Gradually add oil, stirring constantly with fork. Work mixture lightly between finger tips until mixture is the size of small peas. Add softened yeast and mix well. Gradually add 1/4 cup water until dough is slightly sticky to the touch. Let dough stand in warm place until double in size, about 1 hour.

Roll dough out on lightly floured board to 1/8-inch thickness. Cut with floured biscuit cutter and place half the biscuits on non-stick baking sheet. Brush with half the liquid Butter Buds. Stack remaining biscuits on top of first layer. Let rise in warm place 30 to 40 minutes, until double in size. Preheat oven to 350°F. Bake until light brown, 5 to 7 minutes. Brush with remaining Butter Buds; continue baking until golden brown, about 10 minutes.

PER SERVING (1 biscuit):	Calories: 85	Protein: 2gm
Carbohydrate: 13gm	Fat: 2gm	Sodium: 90mg

By using Butter Buds instead of butter in this recipe, you have saved 75 calories and 28 mg cholesterol per serving.

Easter Egg Bread

16 servings

1 package active dry yeast
1/4 cup warm water
1/2 cup milk
1 packet Butter Buds
1/4 cup sugar
3 tablespoons vegetable
  shortening
1 teaspoon salt

1 teaspoon grated orange peel
3 cups all-purpose flour,
  divided
1/2 teaspoon cinnamon
1 egg, slightly beaten
1/3 cup raisins
1/4 cup liquid Butter Buds
  (optional)

Soften yeast in warm water. In saucepan, heat milk, Butter Buds, sugar, shortening, salt, and orange peel until sugar dissolves. Transfer to large bowl and cool until lukewarm. Stir in 1 cup of flour and cinnamon; beat until smooth. Add softened yeast and egg; beat well. Stir in enough remaining flour to make a soft dough. Mix in raisins. Knead on lightly floured surface until smooth and elastic, 8 to 10 minutes. Place in bowl sprayed with non-stick coating agent and turn to coat entire surface. Cover; let rise in warm place, free from draft, until almost double in bulk, about 1 hour.

Punch dough down; divide into thirds. Cover and let rise 10 minutes. Form one-third of dough into 6 egg shapes; place close together in center of non-stick baking sheet. For "egg nest," shape remaining dough into two 26-inch ropes; twist together. Coil around "eggs" and seal ends together. Cover and let rise in warm place until almost double in bulk, about 1 hour. Preheat oven to 375°F. Bake 20 to 25 minutes, or until golden brown. Brush bread with liquid Butter Buds during baking. Remove from baking sheet and cool on wire rack.

PER SERVING (one 1-inch slice):	Calories: 140	Protein: 3gm
Carbohydrate: 24gm	Fat: 3gm	Sodium: 170mg

By using Butter Buds instead of butter in this recipe, you have saved 70 calories and 26 mg cholesterol per serving.

Note: If you don't own a non-stick baking sheet, you can spray your baking sheet with a non-stick coating agent.

Gingerbread

 12 servings

1 egg
3 packets Sweet 'N Low
2 tablespoons margarine
2/3 cup boiling water
1 cup molasses
2 cups sifted all-purpose
flour

2 teaspoons ginger
1 teaspoon baking soda
1/2 teaspoon cinnamon
1/4 teaspoon cloves
1/4 teaspoon salt

Preheat oven to 325°F. In large bowl, beat egg with Sweet 'N Low. Melt margarine in boiling water. Add to egg mixture. Stir in molasses. Sift dry ingredients together; add to egg mixture and beat until smooth. Pour into non-stick 9-inch square baking pan. Bake 40 minutes, or until toothpick inserted in center comes out clean.

PER SERVING (one 2×3-inch piece):	Calories: 165	Protein: 3gm
Carbohydrate: 33gm	Fat: 3gm	Sodium: 170mg

Note: If you don't own a non-stick 9-inch square baking pan, you can spray your baking pan with a non-stick coating agent.

Mixed Corn Bread

 18 servings

4 eggs
1/3 cup vegetable oil
2 cups buttermilk
4 packets Sweet 'N Low
2 teaspoons cream of tartar
1 teaspoon baking soda

1 teaspoon salt
2 cups yellow cornmeal
1/2 cup whole-wheat flour
1/2 cup unprocessed bran
1/2 cup wheat germ
1/2 cup rolled oats

Preheat oven to 425°F. Spray 13×9-inch pan with non-stick coating agent. In large bowl, beat eggs with electric mixer. Stir in oil, buttermilk, Sweet 'N Low, cream of tartar, baking soda, and salt. Combine remaining ingredients, add to liquid, and mix thoroughly. Pour into prepared pan. Bake 25 to 30 minutes, or until toothpick inserted in center comes out clean.

PER SERVING (2×3-inch piece):	Calories: 155	Protein: 5gm
Carbohydrate: 20gm	Fat: 6gm	Sodium: 240mg

Note: There's no need to spray with a non-stick coating agent if you own a non-stick pan.

Applesauce Nut Bread 18 servings

1 cup sifted all-purpose flour	1/2 teaspoon nutmeg
1 cup whole-wheat flour	1/2 teaspoon baking soda
1/3 cup sugar	1 cup chopped walnuts
6 packets Sweet 'N Low	1 egg
1 tablespoon baking powder	1 cup unsweetened applesauce
1/2 teaspoon salt	1/4 cup vegetable oil

Preheat oven to 350°F. Spray 9×5-inch loaf pan with non-stick coating agent. In large bowl, sift together dry ingredients; stir in nuts. In separate bowl, beat egg with electric mixer until frothy, about 30 seconds. Stir in applesauce and oil. Add to dry ingredients and stir just until blended. Pour into prepared pan. Bake 1 hour, or until toothpick inserted in center comes out clean.

PER SERVING (one 1/2-inch slice):	Calories: 140	Protein: 3gm
Carbohydrate: 16gm	Fat: 8gm	Sodium: 140mg

By substituting 1/4 cup liquid Butter Buds for the vegetable oil in this recipe, you can save 25 calories, 3 gm of fat, and 8 mg cholesterol. However, you will add 15 mg of sodium.

Note: There's no need to spray with a non-stick coating agent if you own a non-stick 9×5-inch loaf pan.

Banana Bread 18 servings

1 cup sifted all-purpose flour	1 packet Butter Buds, mixed with 1/4 cup hot water
3/4 cup sifted whole-wheat flour	
2 teaspoons baking powder	
1/4 teaspoon baking soda	1/4 cup sugar
1/4 teaspoon salt	3 packets Sweet 'N Low
1 egg, well beaten	1 teaspoon vanilla
	1 cup mashed bananas

Preheat oven to 350°F. In medium-size bowl, sift together flours, baking powder, baking soda, and salt. In separate bowl, combine egg, Butter Buds, sugar, Sweet 'N Low, vanilla, and bananas. Add dry ingredients, mix until moist. Turn into non-stick 9×5-inch loaf pan. Bake 1 hour, or until toothpick inserted in center comes out clean.

PER SERVING (one 1/2-inch slice):	Calories: 70	Protein: 2gm
Carbohydrate: 15gm	Fat: trace	Sodium: 135mg

By using Butter Buds instead of butter in this recipe, you have saved 42 calories and 16 mg cholesterol per serving.

Carrot Raisin Bread 18 servings

2 eggs
1/4 cup sugar
1/4 cup firmly packed light
    brown sugar
1/4 cup liquid Butter Buds
1 1/4 cups all-purpose flour

1/4 cup rolled oats
2 teaspoons baking powder
1/4 teaspoon salt
1 teaspoon cinnamon
1 cup shredded carrots
1/4 cup raisins

Preheat oven to 350°F. In large bowl, beat eggs with electric mixer until very light and frothy, about 2 minutes. Add sugars and continue beating, about 3 minutes. Blend in Butter Buds. In separate bowl, combine flour, oats, baking powder, salt, and cinnamon. Add gradually to egg mixture. Stir in carrots and raisins. Spray 9×5-inch loaf pan with non-stick coating agent. Bake 45 to 50 minutes, or until toothpick inserted in center comes out clean.

PER SERVING (one 1/2-inch slice):	Calories: 70	Protein: 2gm
Carbohydrate: 14gm	Fat: 1gm	Sodium: 95mg

By using Butter Buds instead of butter in this recipe, you have saved 21 calories and 8 mg cholesterol per serving.

Cranberry Nut Loaf 18 servings

2 1/2 cups sifted all-purpose
    flour
3/4 cup sugar
1/2 cup low-fat milk
1 packet Butter Buds, made
    into liquid

1 egg
3 1/2 teaspoons baking powder
1/2 teaspoon salt
1 cup coarsely chopped
    cranberries
1/4 cup chopped walnuts

Preheat oven to 350°F. In large bowl, combine flour, sugar, milk, Butter Buds, egg, baking powder, and salt. Beat with electric mixer on medium speed 30 seconds, or just until moistened, scraping sides and bottom of bowl. Stir in cranberries and walnuts. Turn batter into non-stick 9×5-inch loaf pan. Bake 55 to 65 minutes, or until toothpick inserted in center comes out clean. Remove from pan; cool thoroughly before slicing.

PER SERVING (one 1/2-inch slice):	Calories: 120	Protein: 3gm
Carbohydrate: 25gm	Fat: 2gm	Sodium: 180mg

By using Butter Buds instead of butter in this recipe, you have saved 42 calories and 16 mg cholesterol per serving.

Energy Bread

 18 servings

1/2 cup chopped dried apricots
1/2 cup raisins
3/4 cup plus 1 tablespoon whole-wheat flour, divided
3/4 cup all-purpose flour
3/4 cup firmly packed light brown sugar
3 1/2 teaspoons baking powder

2 teaspoons cinnamon
1/2 teaspoon ground cloves
1/2 teaspoon salt
2 eggs
1 packet Butter Buds, made into liquid
1 1/2 cups bran cereal
3/4 cup low-fat milk

Preheat oven to 350°F. Toss apricots and raisins with 1 tablespoon whole-wheat flour; set aside. In large bowl, thoroughly combine all-purpose flour, 3/4 cup whole-wheat flour, sugar, baking powder, cinnamon, cloves, and salt. In separate bowl, combine remaining ingredients. Stir into flour mixture just until moistened. Stir in apricots and raisins. Turn batter into non-stick 9×5-inch loaf pan. Bake 1 hour, or until toothpick inserted in center comes out clean. Cool on wire rack 10 minutes. Remove from pan and cool completely.

PER SERVING (one 1/2-inch slice):	Calories: 120	Protein: 3gm
Carbohydrate: 27gm	Fat: 1gm	Sodium: 220mg

By using Butter Buds instead of butter in this recipe, you have saved 42 calories and 16 mg cholesterol per serving.

Note: If you don't own a non-stick 9×5-inch loaf pan, you can spray your loaf pan with a non-stick coating agent.

Buttery Pancake Syrup

 3/4 cup

3/4 cup reduced-calorie maple-flavored syrup

1 packet Butter Buds
1/4 teaspoon cinnamon

Beat Butter Buds into syrup until well blended (Butter Buds won't be dissolved). Transfer to saucepan. Simmer until Butter Buds dissolve, stirring constantly. Add cinnamon and mix well. Serve over pancakes, waffles, or French toast.

PER SERVING (1 tablespoon):	Calories: 70	Protein: 0
Carbohydrate: 16gm	Fat: 0	Sodium: 145mg

By using Butter Buds instead of butter in this recipe, you have saved 63 calories and 23 mg cholesterol per serving.

Appetizers and Beverages

Add good nutrition to any meal with these delicious starters. Entertain guests with Mock Herring (page 48) or a luscious Double Thick Strawberry Shake (page 42). While these recipes sound sinfully fattening, they're no threat to your waistline because you'll save oodles of calories using Butter Buds or Sweet 'N Low instead of butter and sugar.

Holiday Eggnog

 4 servings

1 1/2 cups low-fat milk
1/2 cup evaporated skim milk,
  undiluted
1/2 cup light rum

2 eggs
2 packets Sweet 'N Low
1/2 teaspoon vanilla
4 dashes nutmeg

Combine all ingredients except nutmeg in blender container. Cover and process on low speed about 30 seconds, or until frothy. Pour into cups and sprinkle with nutmeg.

PER SERVING (about 3/4 cup):	Calories: 187	Protein: 9gm
Carbohydrate: 10gm	Fat: 5gm	Sodium: 124mg

Double-Thick Strawberry Shake

 2 servings

1 can (12 ounces) diet cream
  soda
2/3 cup instant non-fat dry
  milk

2 packets Sweet 'N Low
1 teaspoon vanilla
1 cup frozen strawberries

Combine all ingredients except strawberries in blender container. Cover and process on low speed 5 seconds. Add strawberries gradually, processing several seconds between additions. When all strawberries are added, cover blender and process on high 5 to 10 seconds.

PER SERVING (about 1 cup):	Calories: 110	Protein: 8gm
Carbohydrate: 19gm	Fat: trace	Sodium: 120mg

Vanilla Milkshake

 1 serving

1/3 cup instant non-fat dry milk
1 cup ice water

2 packets Sweet 'N Low
1 teaspoon vanilla

Combine all ingredients in blender container. Cover and process at high speed about 30 seconds, or until frothy.

Variations: Substitute 1 teaspoon instant coffee granules for vanilla.

Substitute 1 teaspoon cocoa powder for vanilla.

Add 1/2 cup fresh fruit before processing.

PER SERVING (1 cup):	Calories: 88	Protein: 8gm
Carbohydrate: 13gm	Fat: trace	Sodium: 120mg

Buttered Almond Breakfast Shake

 2 servings

1 1/2 cups low-fat milk
   1 packet Butter Buds, made
      into liquid
   2 eggs

4 teaspoons honey
1/4 teaspoon nutmeg
1/8 teaspoon almond extract

Combine all ingredients in blender container. Cover and process at high speed 30 seconds, or until frothy. Chill. If desired, sprinkle with additional nutmeg.

PER SERVING (1 cup):	Calories: 225	Protein: 12gm
Carbohydrate: 27gm	Fat: 8gm	Sodium: 540mg

By using Butter Buds instead of butter in this recipe, you have saved 376 calories and 140 mg cholesterol per serving.

Nice to know: Drink may also be mixed in a covered jar and shaken vigorously.

Coffee Frost

 1 serving

1/3 cup instant non-fat dry milk
  1 cup strong black coffee,
    chilled

2 packets Sweet 'N Low
  Dash cinnamon

Combine all ingredients in blender container. Cover and process at high speed about 30 seconds, or until light and frothy. Serve over cracked ice.

PER SERVING (about 1 cup):	Calories: 90	Protein: 8gm
Carbohydrate: 13gm	Fat: trace	Sodium: 120mg

Spicy Iced Tea

 4 cups

    4 tea bags
1/2 lemon, cut into slices
  2 packets Sweet 'N Low

3 cinnamon sticks
8 whole cloves
4 cups boiling water

Combine tea bags, lemon, Sweet 'N Low, cinnamon, and cloves in a heat-proof pitcher. Pour in water. Let stand 1 hour, until cooled. Remove tea bags. Chill tea in refrigerator. Strain before serving.

PER SERVING (1 cup):	Calories and nutrients insignificant.

Brandied Coffee

 1 serving

1 packet Sweet 'N Low
1 teaspoon instant decaffein-
    ated coffee
1/2 teaspoon brandy extract

1/2 cup boiling water
2 tablespoons evaporated
    skim milk

Combine Sweet 'N Low, instant coffee, brandy extract, and water. Stir in milk.

PER SERVING (1/2 cup):	Calories: 200	Protein: 2gm
Carbohydrate: 45gm	Fat: trace	Sodium: 70mg

Herb-Stuffed Mushrooms

 6 servings

24 large (1 to 1 1/2 pounds)
    fresh mushrooms
1/2 cup white wine
2 beef-flavor bouillon
    cubes
1/4 cup finely chopped onion

2 packets Butter Buds,
    made into liquid
1/2 cup packaged herb-
    seasoned stuffing mix

Wash mushrooms; remove stems and reserve. In medium-size saucepan, combine wine and bouillon; heat until bouillon dissolves. Add mushroom caps, tops down; cover and simmer 2 to 3 minutes. Remove mushrooms and set aside; reserve wine mixture. Prepare grill for barbecuing. If using a charcoal grill, position rack 2 to 3 inches from coals. If an electric or gas grill is used, cook on medium setting.

Chop mushroom stems. In separate saucepan, combine chopped mushrooms, onion, 1/2 cup Butter Buds, and 1/4 cup wine mixture. Cook over medium heat until vegetables are tender, about 2 to 3 minutes. Stir in stuffing. Place 1 tablespoon stuffing on half of the mushroom caps; top with remaining caps. String caps onto skewers. Turn skewers over hot coals 2 to 3 minutes, brushing occasionally with remaining 1/2 cup Butter Buds.

PER SERVING (2 mushroom cap "sandwiches"):		
Calories: 52	Protein: 2gm	
Carbohydrate: 6gm	Fat: trace	Sodium: 515mg

By using Butter Buds instead of butter in this recipe, you have saved 250 calories and 93 mg cholesterol per serving.

Dippers

 12 servings

1 pound lean flank steak
Freshly ground pepper
to taste
1 pound fresh mushrooms

1 pound fresh string beans
1 pound fresh broccoli
1 medium head (about 1 1/4
pounds) cauliflower

Preheat broiler. Sprinkle steak with pepper. Cut into thin strips and arrange on rack of broiler pan. Broil about 5 minutes, or until done as desired. Wash vegetables well and trim leaves and ends. Slice mushrooms and beans. Cut broccoli and cauliflower into bite-size pieces. Arrange meat and vegetables on serving platter surrounding bowl of Cottage Cheese Dip (below).

PER SERVING (Dippers only):	Calories: 95	Protein: 12gm
Carbohydrate: 8gm	Fat: 2gm	Sodium: 30mg

Cottage Cheese Dip

 1 cup

1 cup low-fat cottage cheese
1 packet Butter Buds
1 tablespoon Worcestershire
sauce
4 teaspoons minced onion

1 teaspoon horseradish
1 teaspoon caraway seeds
Freshly ground pepper
to taste
Dash paprika (optional)

Place cheese in blender container. Cover and process at medium speed 30 seconds, or until smooth. Add Butter Buds, Worcestershire, onion, and horseradish; process 10 seconds, or until well mixed. Scrape into bowl and stir in caraway and pepper. Garnish with paprika. Serve with Dippers.

PER SERVING (2 tablespoons):	Calories: 25	Protein: 4gm
Carbohydrate: 2gm	Fat: trace	Sodium: 185mg

By using Butter Buds instead of butter in this recipe, you have saved 180 calories and 70 mg cholesterol per serving.

Cheese Fondue

BB 3/4 cup

1/2 cup low-fat milk
1 teaspoon cornstarch
1/2 packet (4 teaspoons) Butter Buds
1 tablespoon chopped fresh parsley
White pepper to taste
2 drops hot pepper sauce
1/8 teaspoon garlic powder
1/8 teaspoon marjoram
1/3 cup grated Swiss cheese
1/3 cup grated part-skim mozzarella cheese
1/4 cup white wine
6 ounces (4 to 6 slices) Italian or French bread with hard crust, cut in 1-inch cubes

Combine milk and cornstarch in top of double boiler. Heat over boiling water. Add Butter Buds, parsley, pepper, hot pepper sauce, garlic powder, and marjoram. Blend thoroughly. Add cheeses, stirring constantly until melted. Add wine gradually and stir until smooth. Transfer to fondue pot and keep hot during service. Using fork, dip bread into fondue.

PER SERVING (about 1/3 cup):	Calories: 235	Protein: 10gm
Carbohydrate: 30gm	Fat: 5gm	Sodium: 600mg

By using Butter Buds instead of butter in this recipe, you have saved 190 calories and 70 mg cholesterol per serving.

Swedish Meatballs

 6 servings

1 egg
1 pound very lean ground beef
1/2 pound lean ground pork
1 cup cooked, mashed potatoes
1 packet Sweet 'N Low
1/4 teaspoon allspice
1/4 teaspoon ginger
1/4 teaspoon ground cloves
1/4 teaspoon nutmeg
1/4 teaspoon freshly ground pepper
1/3 cup whole-wheat flour
3/4 cup evaporated skim milk, undiluted

In large mixing bowl, beat egg lightly and combine with remaining ingredients except flour and milk. Form into 30 walnut-size balls. Roll lightly in flour. In medium-size non-stick skillet, brown a few at a time. Preheat oven to 350°F. Transfer meatballs to Dutch oven. Cover with milk. Bake, covered, about 1 hour, or until fully cooked.

PER SERVING (5 meatballs):	Calories: 310	Protein: 30gm
Carbohydrate: 14gm	Fat: 14gm	Sodium: 305mg

Toast Cups

 6 servings

6 slices enriched white
bread

1 packet Butter Buds,
made into liquid

Preheat oven to 350°F. Trim off bread crust. Flatten bread slices
with rolling pin. Spray muffin tin with non-stick coating agent.
Press bread into muffin cups and brush with Butter Buds. Bake
until crusty and golden brown, 10 to 15 minutes. Serve filled
with 1/4 cup Veal Stew with Mushrooms (page 80), Hungarian
Goulash (page 74), or Quick Chicken Stroganoff (page 85).

PER SERVING (one toast cup only):	Calories: 75	Protein: 2gm
Carbohydrate: 13gm	Fat: trace	Sodium: 275mg

*By using Butter Buds instead of butter in this recipe, you have
saved 125 calories and 47 mg cholesterol per serving.*

Note: *There's no need to spray with a non-stick coating agent if
you own non-stick muffin tins.*

Hot Apple-Tomato Appetizer

 4 servings

4 medium-size (about 1 1/4
pounds) ripe tomatoes
2 cups unsweetened apple juice
3 tablespoons liquid Butter
Buds

1 teaspoon lemon juice
8 whole cloves
1/8 teaspoon basil

Soak tomatoes in boiling water until skin cracks, about 30
seconds. Remove stem end and peel. Cut up and place in
blender container. Cover and process on low speed 10 seconds.
Strain. In medium-size saucepan, combine tomatoes, apple
juice, Butter Buds, lemon juice, cloves, and basil. Simmer 5 to 8
minutes. Strain to remove cloves. Serve hot in mugs.

PER SERVING (3/4 cup):	Calories: 95	Protein: 2gm
Carbohydrate: 22gm	Fat: trace	Sodium: 90mg

*By using Butter Buds instead of butter in this recipe, you have
saved 71 calories and 27 mg cholesterol per serving.*

Mock Herring

 About 3 1/2 cups

2 medium onions, sliced
2 stalks celery, cut into
   1-inch pieces
1 small eggplant, peeled and
   cut into long strips,
   1-inch wide

1 cup plain low-fat yogurt
1 tablespoon lemon juice
1 packet Sweet 'N Low
1/4 teaspoon salt
1/8 teaspoon ground cloves
1 bay leaf

Steam onions and celery in vegetable steamer over boiling water 5 to 6 minutes. Add eggplant and steam about 5 minutes, or until soft but not mushy. Remove vegetables to bowl and set aside to cool. In separate bowl, combine remaining ingredients; mix gently with cooled vegetables. Remove bay leaf. Chill thoroughly. Serve on whole-grain bread or crackers.

PER SERVING (1/3 cup):	Calories: 30	Protein: 2gm
Carbohydrate: 6gm	Fat: 1gm	Sodium: 80mg

Barbecued Spareribs

 24 servings

2 pounds pork spareribs
1 cup apple juice
1 tablespoon soy sauce
2 tablespoons hoisin sauce
   or catsup

1 tablespoon honey
1 packet Sweet 'N Low

In large saucepan of boiling water, simmer ribs about 5 minutes to remove excess fat. Drain. In shallow baking dish, combine remaining ingredients. Add ribs and marinate 2 to 3 hours. Preheat oven to 350°F. Bake, uncovered, 45 minutes. Increase temperature to 450°F and continue baking 5 to 10 minutes, or until very tender.

PER SERVING (1 rib):	Calories: 80	Protein: 3gm
Carbohydrate: 3gm	Fat: 6gm	Sodium: 75mg

Paprika Meatballs

 16 meatballs

1 pound lean ground beef
1/3 cup liquid Butter Buds
3 tablespoons minced onion
2 tablespoons fine bread
   crumbs
1/4 teaspoon garlic powder
1/8 teaspoon dry mustard
1/8 teaspoon pepper
1 medium-size ripe tomato,
   chopped

1/2 teaspoon basil
1/4 teaspoon thyme
2 cups low-fat milk,
   divided
1 packet Butter Buds
3 tablespoons all-purpose
   flour
2 teaspoons paprika

In large bowl, combine beef, Butter Buds, onion, bread crumbs, garlic powder, mustard, and pepper and mix thoroughly. Shape mixture into 16 cocktail-size meatballs. Brown in large non-stick skillet over medium heat about 10 to 15 minutes, or until meatballs are browned on all sides. Remove from skillet and drain off excess fat.

Combine tomato, basil, and thyme in same skillet. Cook until tomato is very soft, about 5 to 10 minutes. In saucepan, heat 1 1/2 cups milk until warm. Add Butter Buds and stir until dissolved. Add flour and paprika to remaining milk and stir to a smooth paste. Add to heated milk mixture and blend thoroughly. Slowly add cooked tomato to milk mixture, stirring constantly. Transfer mixture to large skillet and add meatballs. Heat thoroughly just until hot. Do not boil.

PER SERVING (1 meatball):	Calories: 70	Protein: 7gm
Carbohydrate: 4gm	Fat: 3gm	Sodium: 90mg

By using Butter Buds instead of butter in this recipe, you have saved 80 calories and 30 mg cholesterol per serving.

Note: If you don't own a non-stick skillet, you can spray your skillet with a non-stick coating agent.

Stuffed Cabbage

 18 servings

2 medium-size onions, cut in
  chunks
1 large head cabbage
2 pounds lean ground veal or
  beef
Freshly ground pepper
  to taste

1 teaspoon garlic powder
2 cups tomato juice, divided
4 packets Sweet 'N Low
2 tablespoons lemon juice

In large saucepan, cook onions and cabbage in boiling water about 5 minutes. Drain, leaving onions in saucepan and removing cabbage. Mix ground meat with pepper, garlic powder, and 1/2 cup tomato juice. Divide in 18 portions. Separate cabbage leaves and place a portion of meat on each. Roll up and fasten with toothpick. Place in saucepan with onions. Stir Sweet 'N Low and lemon juice into remaining tomato juice. Pour over all. Cover and gently simmer 1 hour, or until cabbage is tender and meat is cooked through.

PER SERVING (1 cabbage roll):	Calories: 110	Protein: 12gm
Carbohydrate: 4gm	Fat: 5gm	Sodium: 100mg

Soups, Salads, and Dressings

Lunch is an important part of every day. Treat yourself to a good one with Cheesy Fish Chowder (page 56) or Chicken Salad (page 62). Add a tossed salad with one of our delicious dressings to any meal. Vegetables and meat have new flavor with Mornay Sauce (page 69) or Barbecue Sauce (page 68). Your meals will have an interesting flair even though you are watching your diet.

Mulligatawny Soup

 8 servings

1 3-pound broiler-fryer, cut up
5 cups homemade chicken stock
1 bay leaf
6 peppercorns
1/3 cup chopped onion
2 stalks celery, chopped
2 medium-size carrots, sliced
2 sprigs fresh parsley, minced
1/2 teaspoon salt
1 packet Butter Buds,
   made into liquid

3 tablespoons cornstarch
1/2 teaspoon ginger
1 teaspoon coriander
1 clove garlic, minced
   Dash cayenne
2 cups low-fat milk
1 packet Butter Buds
   Freshly ground pepper
   to taste
   Lemon slices

Place chicken in large saucepan or dutch oven and add stock. Tie bay leaf and peppercorns in a piece of cheesecloth and add to sauce pan along with onion, celery, carrots, parsley, and salt. Bring to a boil and simmer 30 minutes, or until chicken is cooked and tender. Remove chicken from pot, bone, and cut into bite-size pieces. Return chicken pieces to soup, discarding spices in cheesecloth, and heat to simmering. In separate saucepan, heat liquid Butter Buds and stir in cornstarch, ginger, coriander, garlic, and cayenne until blended. Remove from heat. Slowly add Butter Buds mixture to soup, stirring constantly until soup thickens slightly. Gradually add milk, mixing well. Add dry Butter Buds and season with pepper. Garnish with fresh lemon slices and serve piping hot.

PER SERVING (1 1/4 cups):	Calories: 145	Protein: 17gm
Carbohydrate: 11gm	Fat: 3gm	Sodium: 420mg

By using Butter Buds instead of butter in this recipe, you have saved 188 calories and 70 mg cholesterol per serving.

Borscht

 2 servings

1 can (8 ounces) beets,
   undrained
1/2 cup plain low-fat yogurt

1 tablespoon lemon juice
1 packet Sweet 'N Low

Place all ingredients in blender container. Cover and process at low speed 5 to 10 seconds. Mixture should be chunky. Chill.

PER SERVING (1 cup):	Calories: 73	Protein: 4gm
Carbohydrate: 14gm	Fat: trace	Sodium: 310mg

Old New England Clam Chowder

 5 servings

3 medium-size (about 1 pound)
whole potatoes
1 large onion
2 cups water
1 bay leaf
1/2 teaspoon celery salt
1/4 teaspoon freshly ground
pepper

1 quart low-fat milk
2 tablespoons cornstarch
2 packets Butter Buds
2 cans (6 1/2 ounces each)
minced clams, undrained
Chopped chives

Peel and dice potatoes and onion and place in a large saucepan along with water, bay leaf, celery salt, and pepper. Boil gently until potatoes are tender, 15 to 20 minutes. Reduce heat to simmering. Combine milk, cornstarch, and Butter Buds and add slowly to potato mixture, stirring constantly. Add clams and juice and stir over medium heat until soup begins to boil and thickens slightly. Reduce heat and simmer 5 minutes. Remove bay leaf and garnish with chopped chives before serving.

PER SERVING (1 1/4 cups):	Calories: 230	Protein: 17gm
Carbohydrate: 32gm	Fat: 4gm	Sodium: 675mg

By using Butter Buds instead of butter in this recipe, you have saved 300 calories and 112 mg cholesterol per serving.

Lettuce Soup

 4 servings

3 cups homemade chicken stock
1 1/2 cups water
1 packet Butter Buds
1/4 teaspoon salt
1/4 teaspoon basil
1/4 teaspoon thyme

1/8 teaspoon freshly ground
pepper
1/4 cup diced celery
1/3 cup chopped celery tops
1 cup thinly sliced
iceberg lettuce

Combine chicken stock and water, in medium-size saucepan. Heat to simmering, but do not boil. Add Butter Buds, salt, basil, thyme, pepper, and diced celery. Simmer, covered 5 minutes. Add celery tops and lettuce. Simmer 3 minutes, or until lettuce is just tender. Keep warm, but do not boil.

PER SERVING (3/4 cup):	Calories: 25	Protein: 2gm
Carbohydrate: 3gm	Fat: trace	Sodium: 370mg

By using Butter Buds instead of butter in this recipe, you have saved 188 calories and 70 mg cholesterol per serving.

Creamed Turkey Soup

 5 servings

1 1/2 cups pared diced potatoes
1/2 cup minced onion
1 1/2 cups water
1 packet Butter Buds, made
    into liquid
1 1/4 cups (1/2 10-ounce package)
    frozen peas and carrots
1 cup cooked cubed turkey

1/2 teaspoon salt
1/8 teaspoon freshly
    ground pepper
1/8 teaspoon rubbed sage
1 tablespoon cornstarch
1 package Butter Buds
1 cup low-fat milk

In large saucepan, combine potatoes, onion, water, and liquid Butter Buds. Cook over medium-high heat 20 minutes. Add peas and carrots, turkey, salt, pepper, and sage. Continue cooking 10 minutes, or until vegetables are tender. Reduce heat to simmering. Dissolve cornstarch and dry Butter Buds in a little milk and add slowly to soup with remaining milk, stirring constantly until slightly thickened, about 5 to 7 minutes.

PER SERVING (1 1/4 cups):	Calories: 165	Protein: 15gm
Carbohydrate: 17gm	Fat: 4gm	Sodium: 540mg

By using Butter Buds instead of butter in this recipe, you have saved 150 calories and 56 mg cholesterol per serving.

Cream of Tomato Soup

 6 servings

1 cup instant non-fat dry
    milk
1 can (46 fluid ounces)
    tomato juice, divided
2 tablespoons minced onion
    flakes
2 tablespoons chopped fresh
    parsley

2 teaspoons distilled
    white vinegar
1/2 teaspoon basil
1/2 teaspoon salt
1 bay leaf
2 whole cloves
1 packet Sweet 'N Low

Place milk powder in bowl. Gradually add 1 1/2 cups tomato juice, stirring to form a smooth paste. Set aside. In large saucepan, combine remaining tomato juice and other ingredients, except Sweet 'N Low, and simmer about 5 minutes. Remove bay leaf and cloves. Pour some of the hot liquid into the tomato-milk paste; stir, then pour mixture back into saucepan. Heat slowly, stirring constantly, to serving temperature. Do not boil. Stir in Sweet 'N Low.

PER SERVING (1 cup):	Calories: 95	Protein: 6gm
Carbohydrate: 18gm	Fat: trace	Sodium: 706mg

De-Lish Fish Soup

 6 servings

4 cups water
3/4 teaspoon salt
1 bay leaf
2 pounds fresh fish fillets
  (sole or flounder)
1 cup thinly sliced celery
1 cup thinly sliced carrots
1 can (1 pound) tomatoes

1 cup peeled, diced
  potatoes
4 thinly sliced green
  onions
2 teaspoons dillweed
2 packets Sweet 'N Low
  Freshly ground pepper
  to taste

In large saucepan, bring water to a boil. Add salt, bay leaf, and fish. Gently simmer, uncovered, 10 minutes. Remove fish and set aside. Strain broth and bring to boil again. Add celery, carrots, tomatoes, and potatoes. Cover and simmer 10 minutes, or until vegetables are tender. Flake fish and add to saucepan, with green onions, dillweed, and Sweet 'N Low. Allow to heat through without boiling. Season with pepper.

PER SERVING (1 cup):	Calories: 155	Protein: 24gm
Carbohydrate: 11gm	Fat: 1gm	Sodium: 485mg

Scandinavian Soup

 6 servings

4 ounces lean beef round, cut
  into 1/2-inch cubes
1 teaspoon vegetable oil
1/3 cup diced celery
1 tablespoon finely chopped
  onion
1 small clove garlic, crushed
1 teaspoon salt
1/2 teaspoon thyme
1/4 teaspoon dry mustard

5 cups water
1 bay leaf
1 packet Butter Buds
1/2 cup diagonally sliced
  carrots (1/4-inch thick)
1/8 teaspoon white pepper
1 cup frozen cut green
  beans
3/4 cup uncooked small
  macaroni shells

In large skillet, brown beef in oil 3 to 4 minutes. Add celery, onion, garlic, salt, thyme, and mustard. Cook until celery is tender, about 7 to 8 minutes. Add water, bay leaf, and Butter Buds. Reduce heat and add carrots, pepper, green beans, and macaroni. Simmer 10 minutes, or until vegetables and macaroni are tender. Remove bay leaf before serving.

PER SERVING (1 1/4 cups):	Calories: 125	Protein: 6gm
Carbohydrate: 14gm	Fat: 7gm	Sodium: 482mg

By using Butter Buds instead of butter in this recipe, you have saved 125 calories and 47 mg cholesterol per serving.

Cheesy Fish Chowder

 5 servings

3 medium-size (about 1 pound)
whole potatoes, peeled
and cut up
2/3 cup chopped onions
1/2 cup water
1 packet Butter Buds, made
into liquid
1/4 teaspoon freshly
ground pepper

1/4 teaspoon paprika
3 cups low-fat milk
4 ounces reduced-fat cheese
food, cut up
1 pound cod or flounder
fillets, cut into
small pieces
1 1/2 tablespoons chopped
fresh parsley

In large saucepan, combine potatoes, onions, water, Butter
Buds, pepper, and paprika. Bring to a boil. Reduce heat and
simmer 15 minutes, or until potatoes are tender; do not drain.
In separate saucepan, heat milk with cheese over low heat
about 10 minutes, stirring constantly until cheese has melted.
Do not boil. Add fish to potato mixture and cook until tender,
about 3 minutes. Stir hot cheese mixture into soup and heat just
until hot. Sprinkle with parsley before serving.

PER SERVING (1 1/4 cups):	Calories: 285	Protein: 29gm
Carbohydrate: 28gm	Fat: 6gm	Sodium: 640mg

*By using Butter Buds instead of butter in this recipe, you have
saved 150 calories and 56 mg cholesterol per serving.*

Asparagus Soup

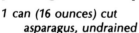 4 servings

1 can (16 ounces) cut
asparagus, undrained
1 chicken-flavor bouillon
cube
1 cup water
2 tablespoons minced onion
flakes

1/2 cup evaporated skim milk,
undiluted
2 tablespoons chopped
fresh parsley
1 packet Sweet 'N Low
Freshly ground pepper
to taste

In medium-size saucepan, combine asparagus with liquid,
bouillon, water, and onion flakes. Simmer about 5 minutes. Stir
in remaining ingredients. Heat but do not boil.

PER SERVING (3/4 cup):	Calories: 60	Protein: 5gm
Carbohydrate: 10gm	Fat: trace	Sodium: 545mg

*Cheesy Fish Chowder, Herb Salad Dressing (page 70),
Paprika Meatballs (page 49).*

Cream of Fresh Tomato Soup

 4 servings

1 1/2 pounds ripe tomatoes
1 tablespoon chopped onion
1 bay leaf
1/8 teaspoon white pepper
3/8 teaspoon thyme, divided
2 tablespoons all-purpose flour

2 cups low-fat milk,
  divided
1 packet Butter Buds,
  made into liquid
1/4 teaspoon basil
1/4 teaspoon sage

Soak tomatoes in boiling water until skin cracks, about 30 seconds. Remove stem ends and peel; chop tomatoes into small pieces. In medium-size saucepan, combine tomatoes, onion, bay leaf, pepper, and 1/4 teaspoon thyme; simmer about 10 minutes. Remove bay leaf. Cool slightly. Pour into blender container and process on low speed 10 to 15 seconds. Strain and keep warm. Add flour to 1/2 cup milk. Mix to a smooth paste. Pour into clean saucepan and add remaining milk and Butter Buds. Cook over low heat, stirring constantly, until thickened. Slowly stir in tomato mixture. Add basil, sage, and remaining 1/8 teaspoon thyme. Heat through.

PER SERVING (1 1/4 cups):	Calories: 105	Protein: 7gm
Carbohydrate: 18gm	Fat: trace	Sodium: 290mg

By using Butter Buds instead of butter in this recipe, you have saved 188 calories and 70 mg cholesterol per serving.

Sunshine Citrus Mold

 10 servings

1 can (8 ounces) juice-
  packed crushed
  pineapple
2 cans (10 1/2 ounces each)
  mandarin orange segments
2 envelopes unflavored
  gelatin

1 packet Sweet 'N Low
1/3 cup chopped walnuts
1 can (12 ounces) diet
  ginger ale, chilled

Drain fruit, reserving juice. In small saucepan, soften gelatin in juice, then heat and stir until gelatin is dissolved. Stir in Sweet 'N Low. Transfer to medium-size bowl and refrigerate about 45 minutes until chilled but not set. Stir in fruit and walnuts. Slowly pour ginger ale down side of bowl; stir gently until blended. Chill until partially set, about 45 minutes. Spoon into individual 1/2-cup molds. Chill until firm, about 1 hour. Unmold.

PER SERVING (1/2 cup):	Calories: 70	Protein: 2gm
Carbohydrate: 9gm	Fat: 3gm	Sodium: 5mg

Dill Marinated Vegetables 6 servings

1 packet Butter Buds, made
    into liquid
1/4 cup red wine vinegar
1 teaspoon dillweed
1 clove garlic, minced
1 tablespoon chopped onion
1/4 teaspoon salt
1/4 teaspoon dry mustard
3 cups (about 12 ounces) fresh
    broccoli, cooked and
    coarsely chopped

1 1/2 cups (3 medium-size)
    coarsely chopped,
    cooked carrots
1 1/2 cups (6 ounces)
    coarsely chopped,
    cooked fresh
    green beans
1 cup (6 ounces) fresh
    mushrooms, cooked
    and sliced

Combine all ingredients except vegetables in covered jar; shake well. Place vegetables in large bowl; add dressing and mix. Cover and chill several hours, stirring occasionally.

PER SERVING (3/4 cup):	Calories: 55	Protein: 4gm
Carbohydrate: 11gm	Fat: trace	Sodium: 265mg

By using Butter Buds instead of butter in this recipe, you have saved 125 calories and 47 mg cholesterol per serving.

Apple Cabbage Slaw 6 servings

1 packet Butter Buds, mixed
    with 1/4 cup water
1/2 cup plain low-fat yogurt
1 tablespoon distilled white
    vinegar
1 tablespoon sugar
3 cups finely shredded
    red cabbage

1 cup chopped green apple,
    unpeeled
1 medium orange, peeled
    and chopped
1/4 cup thinly sliced celery
1/4 cup chopped walnuts

In large bowl, combine Butter Buds, yogurt, vinegar, and sugar. Add remaining ingredients and toss to mix well. Chill.

PER SERVING (2/3 cup):	Calories: 95	Protein: 3gm
Carbohydrate: 14gm	Fat: 3gm	Sodium: 150mg

By using Butter Buds instead of butter in this recipe, you have saved 125 calories and 47 mg cholesterol per serving. If you substitute 1 packet Sweet 'N Low for the sugar in this recipe, you'll save 10 calories.

Cottage Tuna Salad

 4 servings

1 can (6 1/2 ounces) tuna,
    packed in water,
    drained
1 cup low-fat cottage cheese
1/4 cup chopped celery
1/4 cup chopped green onion
2 tablespoons chopped fresh
    parsley

1 tablespoon capers
1/4 cup plain low-fat yogurt
1 tablespoon lemon juice
1/2 teaspoon dry mustard
1 packet Sweet 'N Low
1/4 teaspoon freshly ground
    pepper
1/4 teaspoon salt

In medium bowl, combine tuna, cottage cheese, celery, green onion, parsley, and capers. Mix remaining ingredients in separate bowl. Add to tuna mixture and mix thoroughly. Cover and chill.

PER SERVING (1/2 cup):	Calories: 120	Protein: 21gm
Carbohydrate: 4gm	Fat: 2gm	Sodium: 400mg

Creamy Cucumber Antipasto

 8 servings

1 container (8 ounces) plain
    low-fat yogurt
2 tablespoons distilled white
    vinegar
2 tablespoons chopped fresh
    chives
2 teaspoons dillweed
1 teaspoon celery seed

2 packets Sweet 'N Low
1/2 teaspoon salt
1/2 teaspoon dry mustard
    Dash freshly ground
    pepper
3 medium-size cucumbers,
    peeled and sliced thin

In a bowl, combine all ingredients except cucumbers. Mix thoroughly. Toss cucumber slices in dressing and marinate several hours in refrigerator.

PER SERVING (1/2 cup):	Calories: 25	Protein: 2gm
Carbohydrate: 5gm	Fat: trace	Sodium: 160mg

Carrot Raisin Salad

 4 servings

1/2 cup reduced calorie
    mayonnaise
1 packet Butter Buds
1 teaspoon lemon juice

1/8 teaspoon cinnamon
2 cups (about 6 medium-
    size) grated carrots
1/3 cup raisins

Combine mayonnaise, Butter Buds, lemon juice, and cinnamon; mix well. Add carrots and raisins and mix thoroughly. Chill.

PER SERVING (1/2 cup):	Calories: 150	Protein: 1gm
Carbohydrate: 18gm	Fat: 8gm	Sodium: 250mg

By using Butter Buds instead of butter in this recipe, you have saved 188 calories and 70 mg cholesterol per serving.

Cole Slaw Dressing

 1 1/4 cups

3/4 cup plain low-fat yogurt
1/3 cup malt or red wine vinegar
1/4 cup water

4 packets Sweet 'N Low
1/4 teaspoon salt
Dash freshly ground pepper

Combine all ingredients in bowl and beat with wire whisk. Chill.

PER SERVING (1 tablespoon):	Calories: 5	Protein: trace
Carbohydrate: 1gm	Fat: trace	Sodium: 30mg

Garden Fresh Salad

 8 servings

2 envelopes unflavored gelatin
1 cup water
2 cups tomato juice
3 tablespoons vinegar
    Dash hot pepper sauce
2 packets Sweet 'N Low

1 1/4 cups diced celery,
    cucumber, or green
    pepper
2 tablespoons diced red
    onion

In medium saucepan, soften gelatin in water. Heat and stir until gelatin is completely dissolved. Stir in tomato juice, vinegar, hot pepper sauce, and Sweet 'N Low. Chill, stirring occasionally, about 1 hour, or until mixture is consistency of unbeaten egg whites. Fold in vegetables. Turn into 1-quart mold or bowl and chill until firm.

PER SERVING (1/2 cup):	Calories: 20	Protein: 2gm
Carbohydrate: 3gm	Fat: trace	Sodium: 145mg

Potato Salad

6 servings

1/3 cup reduced calorie
   mayonnaise
1 packet Butter Buds
1 tablespoon lemon juice
1/2 teaspoon celery seed
1/4 teaspoon salt
3 cups (4 medium-size) diced,
   cooked potatoes

3/4 cup (about 3 stalks)
   celery
1/2 cup (1 medium-size)
   chopped sweet red
   pepper
1/4 cup (1 small) chopped
   onion

Combine mayonnaise, Butter Buds, lemon juice, celery seed, and salt. Add potatoes, celery, red pepper, and onion; mix thoroughly. Refrigerate.

PER SERVING (3/4 cup):	Calories: 105	Protein: 2gm
Carbohydrate: 15gm	Fat: 4gm	Sodium: 260mg

By using Butter Buds instead of butter in this recipe, you have saved 125 calories and 47 mg cholesterol per serving.

Yogurt Fruit Salad

 6 servings

1 container (8 ounces) plain
   low-fat yogurt
3 packets Sweet 'N Low
1 tablespoon lemon juice
3 oranges, peeled and
   sectioned

1 medium-size Red
   Delicious apple,
   diced
2 medium-size bananas,
   peeled and sliced
1/2 cup chopped pecans

In large bowl, combine yogurt, Sweet 'N Low, and lemon juice. Add fruit and pecans, tossing to coat thoroughly. Chill.

PER SERVING (3/4 cup):	Calories: 170	Protein: 3gm
Carbohydrate: 24gm	Fat: 8gm	Sodium: 20mg

Chicken Salad

About 6 servings

1 pound (about 3 cups) cut-up,
   cooked chicken
3/4 cup diced avocado
1/2 cup diced celery

1/4 cup toasted slivered almonds
1 1/2 teaspoons minced onion
3/4 cup Cooked Dressing
   (page 63)

In large bowl, combine chicken, avocado, celery, almonds, and onion. Add Cooked Dressing. Toss lightly.

PER SERVING (3/4 cup):	Calories: 215	Protein: 25gm
Carbohydrate: 7gm	Fat: 8gm	Sodium: 310mg

Cooked Dressing

 3/4 cup

1 packet Butter Buds
1/2 teaspoon dry mustard
1/4 teaspoon celery seed
1/8 teaspoon salt
1/8 teaspoon white pepper
1 cup buttermilk, divided

1 tablespoon cornstarch
1/2 teaspoon distilled
white vinegar
1/4 teaspoon prepared
mustard

In top of double boiler, combine Butter Buds, dry mustard, celery seed, salt, and pepper. Add 1/2 cup buttermilk and mix thoroughly. Place over simmering water. Add cornstarch to remaining 1/2 cup buttermilk and blend to a smooth paste. Add to double boiler and stir to blend. Add vinegar and prepared mustard. Heat until mixture thickens, 10 to 15 minutes, stirring constantly. Remove from heat; cool. Refrigerate for 30 minutes before using. Use on meat or fish salads.

PER SERVING (2 tablespoons): Calories: 25	Protein: 1gm
Carbohydrate: 5gm Fat: trace	Sodium: 245mg

By using Butter Buds instead of butter in this recipe, you have saved 63 calories and 23 mg cholesterol per serving.

Mixed Vegetable Slaw

 6 servings

2 1/2 cups shredded green
cabbage
1 cup shredded red cabbage
1/4 cup grated carrot
1/4 cup thinly sliced radish
1 teaspoon chopped onion

1 cup Butter Buds "Mayo"
(page 65)
3 tablespoons plain low-fat yogurt
1/2 teaspoon celery seed
1/4 teaspoon oregano
1/8 teaspoon salt

In medium-size bowl, combine cabbages, carrot, radish, and onion. Toss lightly. In separate bowl, mix Butter Buds "Mayo," yogurt, celery seed, oregano, and salt. Pour over vegetables. Blend thoroughly.

PER SERVING (2/3 cup): Calories: 120	Protein: 3gm
Carbohydrate: 7gm Fat: 9gm	Sodium: 320mg

By using Butter Buds instead of vegetable oil in this recipe, you have saved 230 calories per serving.

Herbed Cucumber Salad 4 servings

1 packet Butter Buds, made
  into liquid
1/4 cup red wine vinegar
1 tablespoon sugar
1/4 teaspoon thyme

1/8 teaspoon tarragon
2 cups (2 medium-size)
  sliced cucumber
1/3 cup thinly sliced onion
4 lettuce leaves

In covered jar, combine Butter Buds, vinegar, sugar, thyme, and tarragon; shake well. Place sliced cucumber and onion in glass bowl. Add dressing and mix well. Chill several hours to marinate. Serve on lettuce leaves.

PER SERVING (1/2 cup):	Calories: 35	Protein: 1gm
Carbohydrate: 8gm	Fat: trace	Sodium: 220mg

Nice to know: You can save 10 calories and 3 gm carbohydrate per serving by substituting 1 packet Sweet 'N Low for the sugar in this recipe.

Sodium-Free Spice and Herb Blends 2 to 3 tablespoons

Blend #1 (for vegetables and meat):

1 teaspoon thyme
1 teaspoon marjoram

3/4 teaspoon rosemary
1/2 teaspoon sage

Blend #2 (for vegetables, poultry, and meat):

3/4 teaspoon marjoram
1/2 teaspoon thyme
1/2 teaspoon oregano

1/2 teaspoon sage
1/2 teaspoon rosemary

Blend #3 (for fish):

3/4 teaspoon parsley flakes
1/2 teaspoon onion powder
1/2 teaspoon sage

1/4 teaspoon marjoram
1/4 teaspoon paprika

Blend #4 (for meat, potatoes, and vegetables):

1 teaspoon dry mustard
1/2 teaspoon sage

1/2 teaspoon thyme
1/4 teaspoon marjoram

PER SERVING (1/8 teaspoon):	Calories and nutrients negligible

Note: In each recipe, ground spices and herbs should be used. Store in empty spice bottles with small-holed shaker tops.

Butter Buds "Mayo"

 1 cup

1 packet Butter Buds
1/4 cup instant non-fat dry milk
2 tablespoons hot water
1 egg white
1 tablespoon distilled white
    vinegar

1/2 teaspoon dry mustard
1/4 teaspoon salt
1/4 cup vegetable oil

In small bowl, combine Butter Buds, milk, and water. In separate bowl, beat egg white until foamy. Blend in vinegar, mustard, and salt. While beating, slowly add oil, then contents of first bowl. Chill at least 1 hour. Use as base for dressings and dips.

PER SERVING (2 tablespoons):	Calories: 76		Protein: 1gm
Carbohydrate: 2gm	Fat: 7gm		Sodium: 195mg

By using Butter Buds instead of vegetable oil in this recipe, you have saved 114 calories per serving.

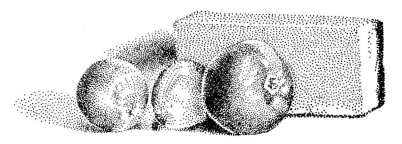

Bleu Cheese
Vinaigrette Dressing

 About 3/4 cup

1 packet Butter Buds, made
    into liquid
1 tablespoon distilled white
    vinegar
1 tablespoon chopped onion

1/8 teaspoon oregano
1/8 teaspoon basil
Dash pepper
2 ounces (about 1/3 cup)
    crumbled bleu cheese

Combine all ingredients except cheese in small jar; cover and shake to mix well. Add cheese; chill.

PER SERVING (1 tablespoon):	Calories: 45		Protein: 2gm
Carbohydrate: 1gm	Fat: 3gm		Sodium: 145mg

By using Butter Buds instead of butter in this recipe, you have saved 63 calories and 23 mg cholesterol per serving.

Clam Sauce for Pasta
 About 2/3 cup

1 packet Butter Buds, made
 into liquid
1 can (6 1/2 ounces) minced
 clams, drained

1 tablespoon chopped
 fresh parsley
1 large clove garlic,
 minced

Combine all ingredients in small saucepan. Heat to simmering.
Serve over spaghetti.

PER SERVING (1/3 cup):	Calories: 75	Protein: 8gm
Carbohydrate: 4gm	Fat: 1gm	Sodium: 500mg

*By using Butter Buds instead of vegetable oil in this recipe, you
have saved 456 calories per serving.*

Tartar Dressing
 About 1 cup

1 cup Butter Buds "Mayo"
 (page 65)
1 small dill pickle, finely
 chopped
1 tablespoon dehydrated chives

1 tablespoon finely chopped
 capers (optional)
1 tablespoon chopped fresh
 parsley (optional)

Combine Butter Buds "Mayo" with remaining ingredients.
Chill. Serve with fish or snacks.

PER SERVING (1 tablespoon):	Calories: 40	Protein: 1gm
Carbohydrate: 1gm	Fat: 3gm	Sodium: 155mg

*By using Butter Buds instead of vegetable oil in this recipe, you
have saved 55 calories per serving.*

Marinara Sauce
2 cups

2 cans (8 ounces each) tomato
 sauce
1 tablespoon chopped fresh
 parsley
1 large clove garlic, crushed

1/2 teaspoon oregano
1/2 teaspoon basil
 Freshly ground pepper
 to taste
1 packet Sweet 'N Low

In medium saucepan, combine all ingredients except Sweet 'N
Low. Cover; simmer over low heat about 10 minutes. Stir in
Sweet 'N Low. Serve with noodles, poultry, and meat.

PER SERVING (2 tablespoons):	Calories: 15	Protein: trace
Carbohydrate: 3gm	Fat: trace	Sodium: 145mg

Creamy French Dressing

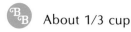 About 1/3 cup

1/3 cup plain low-fat yogurt
1 packet Butter Buds
1 tablespoon red wine vinegar
1 teaspoon sugar

3/4 teaspoon paprika
1/8 teaspoon dry mustard
1/8 teaspoon garlic powder

Combine all ingredients and mix well. Chill.

PER SERVING (1 tablespoon): Calories: 20		Protein: 1gm
Carbohydrate: 2gm	Fat: trace	Sodium: 85mg

By using Butter Buds instead of butter in this recipe, you have saved 142 calories and 53 mg cholesterol per serving. You can also substitute 1/2 packet Sweet 'N Low for the sugar in this recipe and save 3 calories and 1 gm carbohydrate per serving.

Low-Sodium Tomato Sauce

 1 1/2 cups

2 teaspoons vegetable oil
2 tablespoons chopped green
    onion, including tops
1 tablespoon chopped green
    pepper
1 small clove garlic, minced
2 tablespoons diced celery
1 pound (about 3 medium-size)
    ripe tomatoes
1/4 cup liquid Butter Buds

1/2 teaspoon oregano
1/2 teaspoon basil
1/4 teaspoon freshly ground
    pepper
1/4 teaspoon sage
1/4 teaspoon thyme
1/4 cup red wine
1 tablespoon all-purpose
    flour
1/2 cup water

Heat oil in large skillet. Sauté green onion, green pepper, garlic, and celery until tender, but not brown. Soak tomatoes in boiling water until skin cracks, about 30 seconds. Remove stem ends and peel. Chop tomatoes and add to skillet with Butter Buds, seasonings, and wine. Blend well. Mix flour with water into a smooth paste. Stir into tomato mixture. Simmer, covered, 25 to 30 minutes, stirring occasionally.

PER SERVING (about 1/3 cup): Calories: 55		Protein: 1gm
Carbohydrate: 8gm	Fat: 2gm	Sodium: 120mg

By using Butter Buds instead of vegetable oil in this recipe, you have saved 55 calories per serving.

Russian Dressing

 About 1 1/4 cups

1 cup Butter Buds "Mayo" (page 65)
1/3 cup catsup
1 tablespoon minced onion
1 teaspoon Worcestershire sauce

2 tablespoons chopped green pepper
2 tablespoons pimiento or chopped red pepper

Combine all ingredients and mix well. Chill. Use as dressing or dip.

PER SERVING (1 tablespoon):	Calories: 35	Protein: 1gm
Carbohydrate: 2gm	Fat: 3gm	Sodium: 130mg

By using Butter Buds instead of vegetable oil in this recipe, you have saved 45 calories per serving.

Homemade Catsup

About 3 1/2 cups

3 cans (1 pound each) whole tomatoes
1/4 cup malt or red wine vinegar
1/4 cup finely chopped onion

2 tablespoons Worcestershire sauce
1/2 teaspoon salt
1 clove garlic, crushed
2 packets Sweet 'N Low

Place contents of 1 can of tomatoes in blender container. Cover and process on medium speed 30 to 40 seconds, or until smooth. Repeat with each can of tomatoes separately. In large saucepan, combine tomatoes with all remaining ingredients except Sweet 'N Low. Simmer, uncovered, until sauce is reduced and thickened, 30 to 40 minutes. Stir in Sweet 'N Low.

PER SERVING (1 tablespoon):	Calories: 6	Protein: trace
Carbohydrate: 1gm	Fat: trace	Sodium: 60mg

Barbecue Sauce

 2 cups

1 1/2 cups tomato juice
1/2 cup cider vinegar
1 packet Butter Buds, mixed with 1/4 cup hot water
1 1/2 tablespoons Worcestershire sauce
2 teaspoons salt

3 cloves garlic, crushed
1 bay leaf
1/4 teaspoon dry mustard
1/4 teaspoon cayenne
Freshly ground pepper to taste
1 packet Sweet 'N Low

In medium saucepan, combine all ingredients except Sweet 'N Low. Bring to a boil and cook 10 minutes. Stir in Sweet 'N Low. Use as marinade or sauce for meats.

PER SERVING (1/4 cup):	Calories: 20	Protein: trace
Carbohydrate: 4gm	Fat: trace	Sodium: 770mg

By using Butter Buds instead of vegetable oil in this recipe, you have saved 114 calories per serving.

Basic White Sauce

 About 2 cups

2 cups low-fat milk
3 tablespoons all-purpose flour
1 packet Butter Buds

Freshly ground pepper
to taste

Combine milk, flour, and Butter Buds in small saucepan. Heat, stirring constantly, until thickened. Season with pepper. Use for creamed chicken, tuna, and chipped beef.

PER SERVING (1/4 cup):	Calories: 55	Protein: 3gm
Carbohydrate: 6gm	Fat: 1gm	Sodium: 150mg

By using Butter Buds instead of butter in this recipe, you have saved 94 calories and 35 mg cholesterol per serving.

Mornay Sauce

 About 2 cups

1 cup grated Cheddar or
American cheese
3/4 teaspoon dry mustard
1/2 teaspoon Worcestershire
sauce

2 cups Basic White Sauce
(above)

Combine all ingredients and blend well. Serve over vegetables, macaroni, or toast.

PER SERVING (1/4 cup):	Calories: 105	Protein: 6gm
Carbohydrate: 8gm	Fat: 5gm	Sodium: 275mg

By using Butter Buds instead of butter in the Basic White Sauce, you have saved 45 calories and 18 mg cholesterol per serving.

Teriyaki Sauce

 2 1/2 cups

1/4 cup soy sauce
2 tablespoons cornstarch
1 cup beef-flavored bouillon
1 cup unsweetened pineapple
  juice
1/4 cup sherry

1 large clove garlic,
  minced
1 teaspoon minced fresh
  ginger (optional)
4 packets Sweet 'N Low

In medium-size saucepan, combine soy sauce and cornstarch. Add remaining ingredients except Sweet 'N Low. Bring to a boil and stir until thickened. Remove from heat and stir in Sweet 'N Low. Serve with meat or poultry.

PER SERVING (2 tablespoons): Calories: 20		Protein: trace
Carbohydrate: 3gm	Fat: trace	Sodium: 315mg

Sauce Velouté

 About 2 cups

1 packet Butter Buds
3 tablespoons all-purpose
  flour

2 cups beef consomme or
  bouillon
Freshly ground pepper
  to taste

Combine all ingredients in small saucepan. Heat stirring constantly, until thickened. Serve with beef or lamb.

PER SERVING (1/4 cup):	Calories: 15	Protein: trace
Carbohydrate: 4gm	Fat: trace	Sodium: 230mg

By using Butter Buds instead of butter in this recipe, you have saved 94 calories and 35 mg cholesterol per serving.

Herb Salad Dressing

 About 2/3 cup

1 packet Butter Buds, made
  into liquid
1 tablespoon distilled white
  vinegar
1 tablespoon lemon juice
1/4 teaspoon garlic powder

1/4 teaspoon oregano
1/4 teaspoon tarragon
1/4 teaspoon thyme
1/8 teaspoon freshly ground
  pepper

Combine all ingredients in small jar; cover and shake until well blended. Serve over your favorite tossed green salad.

PER SERVING (1 tablespoon):	Calories: 5	Protein: trace
Carbohydrate: 1gm	Fat: trace	Sodium: 85mg

Main Dishes

Plan an elegant dinner party with Shrimp de Jonghe (page 98) or Coq Au Vin (page 90). Or enjoy an outdoor barbecue with Teriyaki Beef Kabobs (page 76) Lemon Barbecued Chicken (page 86) or New England Style Clambake (page 96). You'll provide flavors your guests will savor with no concern about extra calories, because each of these delicious dishes is made with Butter Buds instead of butter.

Chili Con Carne

 10 servings

1 1/3 cups (about 8 ounces)
dried kidney beans
5 cups water, divided
1 bay leaf
1 dried chili pepper
1 1/2 pounds lean ground beef
1/2 cup (1 medium-size)
chopped onion
1/2 cup (1 small) chopped
green pepper
1 large clove garlic, minced

1/8 teaspoon cayenne
1/2 teaspoon oregano
1 teaspoon cumin
1/4 cup chopped fresh parsley
1 packet Butter Buds
2 pounds (about 6
medium-size) ripe
tomatoes, chopped
1 can (6 ounces) salt-free
tomato paste

Wash kidney beans and remove blemished ones. Place in large saucepan with 4 cups water, bay leaf, and chili pepper. Boil 2 minutes; reduce heat to simmering. Cover and simmer until beans are tender, about 2 hours. Remove bay leaf. Brown beef, onions, and green pepper in large skillet. Drain excess fat. Add to cooked beans. Add garlic, cayenne, oregano, cumin, parsley, Butter Buds, tomatoes, tomato paste, and remaining 1 cup water to bean mixture. Cover and simmer 1 hour, stirring occasionally.

PER SERVING (1 cup):	Calories: 240	Protein: 21gm
Carbohydrate: 23gm	Fat: 7gm	Sodium: 150mg

By using Butter Buds instead of vegetable oil in this recipe, you have saved 90 calories per serving.

Beef and Cabbage Casserole

 4 servings

1 pound lean ground beef
1 medium-size onion, chopped
3 cups finely shredded
cabbage
1 can (8 ounces) tomato sauce

1/2 cup uncooked long grain
rice
2 packets Sweet 'N Low
1 1/4 cups water

Preheat oven to 350°F. In medium-size non-stick skillet, brown beef and onion; drain fat. Transfer beef and onion to 2 1/2-quart casserole and combine with remaining ingredients. Bake, covered, about 45 minutes.

PER SERVING (1 1/4 cups):	Calories: 320	Protein: 27gm
Carbohydrate: 30gm	Fat: 10gm	Sodium: 460mg

Note: If you don't own a non-stick skillet, you can spray your skillet with a non-stick coating agent.

Picadilly Pie

 6 servings

1 1/4 pounds lean beef round,
cut into 1-inch cubes
1 tablespoon vegetable oil
1/2 teaspoon basil
1/4 teaspoon salt
1/8 teaspoon freshly ground
pepper
1/4 cup white wine
2 cups water

1 1/4 cups whole small onions
or onion wedges
1 1/4 cups (1/2 10-ounce
package) frozen cut
green beans
1 bay leaf
1 packet Butter Buds
2 teaspoons all-purpose
flour

In large skillet, brown beef in oil. Add basil, salt, pepper, and wine. Simmer in covered skillet until almost tender, about 35 minutes. Meanwhile, in medium-size saucepan, heat water to boiling. Add onions, green beans, and bay leaf; heat until vegetables are tender and crisp. Drain, reserving 1 1/4 cups vegetable liquid. Remove bay leaf. Keep vegetables warm. Add reserved liquid, Butter Buds, and flour to beef cubes in skillet. Blend well. Add vegetables and simmer about 7 minutes.

PER SERVING (3/4 cup):	Calories: 255	Protein: 23gm
Carbohydrate: 20gm	Fat: 9gm	Sodium: 285mg

By using Butter Buds instead of butter in this recipe, you have saved 125 calories and 46 mg cholesterol per serving.

Sloppy Disco-Joe

 4 servings

1 pound lean ground beef or
veal
1/2 cup diced onion
1 1/2 cups tomato juice
1/4 teaspoon salt
1 clove garlic, crushed
1/4 teaspoon oregano

1/4 teaspoon basil
1/4 teaspoon turmeric
1/4 teaspoon thyme
Freshly ground pepper
to taste
1 packet Sweet 'N Low

In large non-stick skillet, brown beef and onion. Drain fat. Add all remaining ingredients, except Sweet 'N Low. Simmer, uncovered, about 12 to 15 minutes, until sauce has thickened. Stir in Sweet 'N Low.

PER SERVING (3/4 cup):	Calories: 220	Protein: 24gm
Carbohydrate: 6gm	Fat: 10gm	Sodium: 375mg

Note: If you don't own a non-stick skillet, you can spray your skillet with a non-stick coating agent.

Hungarian Goulash

 6 servings

1 1/2 pounds cubed lean beef
2 medium onions, sliced
1 can (1 pound) whole tomatoes
1 can (8 ounces) tomato sauce
1 1/2 tablespoons paprika
1 packet Sweet 'N Low

Freshly ground pepper
to taste
3 cups cooked (6 ounces
uncooked) whole-wheat or
spinach noodles
1 cup plain low-fat yogurt

In medium-size non-stick saucepan, brown beef on all sides. Remove beef and set aside. In same saucepan, cook onions until transparent. Return beef to pan and add tomatoes, tomato sauce, paprika, Sweet 'N Low, and pepper. Cover and simmer over very low heat 1 hour. Uncover slightly and let simmer 30 minutes, or until meat is tender and sauce has reduced a little. Meanwhile, prepare noodles according to package direction, omitting salt. Remove goulash from heat. Stir in yogurt. Reheat to serving temperature without boiling. Serve over hot noodles.

PER SERVING (1 1/4 cups):	Calories: 230	Protein: 19gm
Carbohydrate: 27gm	Fat: 5gm	Sodium: 490mg

Note: If you don't own a non-stick saucepan, you can spray your saucepan with a non-stick coating agent.

Easy Skillet Dinner

 4 servings

1 pound lean ground beef or
veal
1/2 medium-size onion, sliced
1 cup shredded cabbage
1 cup beef-flavor bouillon
1/2 cup chopped green onion
2 stalks celery, sliced

1 clove garlic, crushed
1 teaspoon soy sauce
1 ounce uncooked spaghetti
1 cup (1/2 10-ounce package)
frozen mixed vegetables
2 packets Sweet 'N Low

Brown beef and onion in large non-stick skillet. Add cabbage, bouillon, green onion, celery, garlic, and soy sauce. Bring to a boil; add spaghetti. Cover and slowly simmer 20 to 25 minutes. Stir in frozen vegetables and Sweet 'N Low. Simmer, uncovered, 5 minutes.

PER SERVING (1 1/2 cups):	Calories: 270	Protein: 27gm
Carbohydrate: 17gm	Fat: 10gm	Sodium: 465mg

Note: If you don't own a non-stick skillet, you can spray your skillet with a non-stick coating agent.

California Pot Roast 8 servings

1 3-pound chuck roast, trimmed
  of excess fat
2 tablespoons all-purpose flour
1 teaspoon salt
  Freshly ground pepper to taste
1 tablespoon vegetable oil
1 large onion, quartered
2 large carrots, sliced in
  1-inch pieces

1 tablespoon Worcester-
  shire sauce
2 cloves garlic, crushed
2 packets Sweet 'N Low
1 bay leaf
1 cup water

Dredge meat in flour, salt, and pepper. Brown in oil in heavy saucepan or dutch oven. Add remaining ingredients. Cover and simmer very slowly over low heat, about 3 hours, or until meat is very tender.

PER SERVING (two 1/2-inch slices): Calories: 235	Protein: 30gm
Carbohydrate: 5gm Fat: 11gm	Sodium: 370mg

Marinated Pork Chops 4 servings

1 packet Butter Buds, mixed
  with 1/4 cup hot water
1/4 cup red wine
  3 tablespoons chopped onion
  2 teaspoons freshly squeezed
    lemon juice with pulp
1 bay leaf
1 large clove garlic, crushed

1/4 teaspoon crushed rosemary
1/4 teaspoon thyme
1/4 teaspoon dry mustard
1/8 teaspoon freshly ground
    pepper
  4 pork chops (about 1 1/2
    pounds)

Combine all ingredients, except pork chops and blend thoroughly. Pour into large, shallow glass bowl. Marinate pork chops, completely covered, 4 to 6 hours or overnight. Preheat oven to 350°F. Remove chops from marinade and bake in square baking dish 20 to 25 minutes or cook outdoors on charcoal grill.

PER SERVING (1 pork chop): Calories: 200	Protein: 22gm
Carbohydrate: 4gm Fat: 10gm	Sodium: 275mg

By using Butter Buds instead of vegetable oil in this recipe, you have saved 228 calories per serving.

Teriyaki Beef Kabobs 4 servings

1 packet Butter Buds, made
  into liquid
2 tablespoons dry sherry
1 tablespoon lemon juice
1 tablespoon soy sauce
2 teaspoons sugar
1 clove garlic, minced
1/4 teaspoon ginger
1 pound top round beef, cut
  into 1 1/2-inch chunks

1 medium-size green pepper,
  seeded and cut into
  1-inch chunks
1 can (8 ounces) juice-packed
  pineapple chunks, drained
1 medium-size onion, cut
  into 1-inch chunks

In medium-size bowl, combine Butter Buds, sherry, lemon juice, soy sauce, sugar, garlic, and ginger. Add beef and stir to coat thoroughly. Cover and refrigerate 2 to 3 hours, stirring occasionally.

Remove beef cubes and reserve marinade. Thread beef, green pepper, pineapple, and onion alternately on four 10-inch wood or metal skewers. Cook 10 to 15 minutes on preheated barbecue grill, turning once during cooking and basting several times with marinade.

PER SERVING (1 skewer):	Calories: 265	Protein: 25gm
Carbohydrate: 17gm	Fat: 10gm	Sodium: 615mg

By using Butter Buds instead of vegetable oil in this recipe, you have saved 228 calories per serving.

Nice to know: One packet of Sweet 'N Low will work just as well in this recipe instead of 2 teaspoons sugar. You'll save 5 calories and 2 gm carbohydrate per serving.

Marinated Pork Chops (page 75), Teriyaki Beef Kabobs.

Herbed Hamburgers

 4 servings

1 pound lean ground beef
1/4 cup liquid Butter Buds
2 tablespoons chopped fresh
  parsley
2 tablespoons fine bread crumbs
2 teaspoons chopped pimiento

2 teaspoons finely chopped
  onion
1/4 teaspoon oregano
1/4 teaspoon garlic powder
1/4 teaspoon salt

Mix all ingredients. Hand-mold into 4 patties. Broil until done as desired, about 7 to 10 minutes, turning once. Do not overcook.

PER SERVING (1 patty):	Calories: 210	Protein: 25gm
Carbohydrate: 4gm	Fat: 10gm	Sodium: 350mg

By using Butter Buds instead of butter in this recipe, you have saved 94 calories and 35 mg cholesterol per serving.

Peachy Pork Chops

 6 servings

6 lean pork chops (about
  2 pounds)
1/2 teaspoon freshly ground
  pepper
1 can (1 pound) juice-packed
  peach halves
3 packets Sweet 'N Low

2 teaspoons lemon juice
1/4 teaspoon cinnamon
1/4 teaspoon ginger
3 whole cloves
2 teaspoons all-purpose
  flour

Carefully trim away any visible fat from chops. Season chops with pepper and brown in large non-stick skillet. Drain off fat. Drain peaches, reserving 1/2 cup juice. Combine juice with Sweet 'N Low, lemon juice, and spices. Pour over pork; cover tightly. Simmer gently over very low heat, about 45 minutes, or until pork is well cooked, turning chops once. Remove chops to serving platter and keep warm. Add peaches to liquid in skillet. Cover and heat through, about 5 minutes. Place one peach half on each chop. Mix flour with remaining juice and stir into pan juices. Heat and stir until sauce thickens, about 5 minutes. Remove cloves. Pour sauce over chops.

PER SERVING (1 pork chop):	Calories: 180	Protein: 18gm
Carbohydrate: 7gm	Fat: 9gm	Sodium: 400mg

Note: If you don't own a non-stick skillet, you can spray your skillet with a non-stick coating agent.

Pork and Apple Loaf 8 servings

1 1/2 pounds lean ground pork
1 medium-size onion, finely
    chopped
1 clove garlic, crushed
1/3 cup coarsely chopped walnuts
1 teaspoon grated lemon peel
2 medium-size apples, peeled
    cored, and finely chopped
2 tablespoons lemon juice
1 1/2 cups cubed fresh whole-
    wheat bread, crusts removed

1/2 cup chicken-flavored
    bouillon
2 eggs, beaten
1 teaspoon salt
1 packet Sweet 'N Low
1/4 teaspoon rosemary
1/4 teaspoon sage
1/4 teaspoon thyme
1/8 teaspoon nutmeg
    Chopped fresh parsley

Preheat oven to 350°F. In large bowl, combine pork, onion, garlic, walnuts, and lemon peel. In separate bowl, toss apples in lemon juice and add to pork mixture. Soak bread in bouillon. Add to pork with eggs, salt, Sweet 'N Low, and seasonings. Thoroughly mix all ingredients, mold into 12-inch loaf, and place in shallow roasting pan. Bake, uncovered, 1 hour to 1 hour 15 minutes, or until loaf is brown and juices run clear when pricked. Let stand 10 minutes. Pour off fat. Sprinkle top with parsley.

PER SERVING (1-inch slice): Calories: 215	Protein: 16gm
Carbohydrate: 12gm Fat: 12gm	Sodium: 445mg

Orange Barbecued Pork 4 servings

1 teaspoon cornstarch
1 packet Butter Buds, made
    into liquid
1/3 cup frozen orange juice
    concentrate, undiluted

1/8 teaspoon cinnamon
1/8 teaspoon ground cloves
1 pound lean, boneless
    pork tenderloin

Dissolve cornstarch in Butter Buds. Add orange juice, cinnamon, and cloves. Mix well. Pour over pork and refrigerate, covered, 1 to 2 hours. Remove meat from marinade and reserve. Place pork on preheated barbecue grill. Cook about 15 minutes each side, basting occasionally with reserved marinade, or until meat thermometer registers 180°F to 185°F.

PER SERVING (two 1/2-inch slices):	Calories: 210	Protein: 19gm
Carbohydrate: 11gm Fat: 9gm		Sodium: 265mg

By using Butter Buds instead of vegetable oil in this recipe, you have saved 228 calories per serving.

Tangy Glazed Ham

 10 servings

1 5-pound lean fresh ham
2 teaspoons cornstarch
1/2 cup unsweetened pineapple
   juice
1 packet Butter Buds, made
   into liquid
1 tablespoon firmly packed
   light brown sugar

1/8 teaspoon ground cloves
1/8 teaspoon allspice
1/2 cup canned juice-packed
   crushed pineapple,
   including juice

Preheat oven to 450°F. Trim ham of all visible fat and place in large roasting pan. Reduce heat to 350°F and bake 1 1/2 hours. Meanwhile, dissolve cornstarch in pineapple juice. Combine with Butter Buds, brown sugar, cloves, and allspice in small saucepan; mix well. Heat until mixture thickens. Add pineapple and spoon glaze over ham. Bake 1 to 1 1/2 hours, brushing occasionally with glaze, until ham reaches an internal temperature of 185°F.

PER SERVING (4 ounces):	Calories: 230	Protein: 30gm
Carbohydrate: 3gm	Fat: 10gm	Sodium: 160mg

By using Butter Buds instead of butter in this recipe, you have saved 75 calories and 28 mg cholesterol per serving.

Veal Stew with Mushrooms

 4 servings

1 pound boneless veal,
   cubed
1 1/4 cups water
1 small onion, pierced with
   5 cloves
1/4 teaspoon salt
1 bay leaf
1/2 cup sliced carrot

2 medium onions,
   cut into wedges
1 1/2 cups (5 ounces) sliced
   fresh mushrooms
1 teaspoon lemon juice
1 packet Butter Buds,
   made into liquid
1 egg, well beaten

In large saucepan or dutch oven, combine veal, water, onion with cloves, salt, and bay leaf. Cover and simmer about 1 hour 15 minutes, or until meat is tender. Remove meat and reserve. Strain broth and pour back into dutch oven. Add carrot and onion wedges and cook about 10 minutes. Add mushrooms and simmer 7 minutes. Drain broth into small saucepan. Add vegetables to meat. Heat broth over medium-high heat about 15 minutes, or until reduced to about 1/3 to 1/2 cup. In large skillet, combine broth, lemon juice, Butter Buds, and egg. Heat on low, stirring constantly, until mixture is slightly thickened. Do not overcook. Add vegetables and meat to sauce. Heat thoroughly but do not boil.

PER SERVING (1 1/4 cups):	Calories: 250		Protein: 25gm
Carbohydrate: 12gm	Fat: 11gm		Sodium: 440mg

By using Butter Buds instead of butter in this recipe, you have saved 188 calories and 70 mg cholesterol per serving.

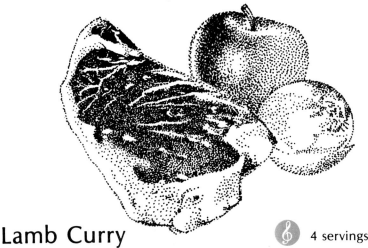

Lamb Curry

4 servings

1 medium-size onion, diced
1 tablespoon vegetable oil
1 1/2 pounds lean lamb, cubed
2 tablespoons all-purpose flour
1 or 2 teaspoons curry powder
1/4 teaspoon ginger

1 medium-size apple, peeled
  and diced
1 cup beef-flavored bouillon
2 tablespoons raisins
1 tablespoon chutney
1 packet Sweet 'N Low
1/2 cup plain low-fat yogurt

In medium saucepan, sauté onion in vegetable oil. Dredge lamb cubes in flour. Add to saucepan and cook 3 to 4 minutes, or until lightly browned. Add curry powder and ginger. Stir and continue cooking 1 minute. Add apple, bouillon, raisins, and chutney. Cover and simmer gently 1 1/2 hours, or until very tender. Add 1/4 cup water if necessary. Stir in Sweet 'N Low and yogurt. Serve over hot cooked rice with assorted condiments, such as chopped raw vegetables and fruits (green pepper, cucumber, tomato, banana, or raisins).

PER SERVING (1 cup):	Calories: 300		Protein: 26gm
Carbohydrate: 17gm	Fat: 13gm		Sodium: 320mg

82

Chicken and Broccoli with Mushroom Sauce

4 servings

1 package (10 ounces) frozen broccoli spears
1 packet Butter Buds, made into liquid
1/4 cup all-purpose flour
1 cup chicken broth
1 can (4 ounces) mushroom slices, drained
1/4 cup white wine
1/4 teaspoon thyme
Dash freshly ground pepper
1 pound cooked chicken, sliced or cubed
2 tablespoons unseasoned bread crumbs
2 tablespoons chopped fresh parsley

Cook broccoli according to package directions, omitting salt. Combine Butter Buds and flour in saucepan and cook over medium heat, 1 to 2 minutes. Blend in chicken broth, stirring constantly until thickened and smooth. Blend in mushrooms, wine, thyme, and pepper. Preheat oven to 375°F. Arrange broccoli in shallow baking pan. Cover with chicken and pour mushroom sauce over all. Top with bread crumbs. Bake, uncovered, 15 to 25 minutes, or until browned and bubbly. Sprinkle with parsley.

PER SERVING (1 cup):	Calories: 265	Protein: 40gm
Carbohydrate: 16gm	Fat: 4gm	Sodium: 795mg

Chicken Italiano

 6 servings

3 whole chicken breasts, halved and skinned
2 cans (6 ounces each) tomato sauce
2 medium-size carrots, thinly sliced
1/4 cup (1/2 medium-size) diced onion
1/2 cup green pepper seeded and diced
2 tablespoons lemon juice
1 clove garlic, crushed
1/2 teaspoon basil
1/4 teaspoon oregano
1/4 teaspoon salt
Freshly ground pepper to taste
1/2 pound mushrooms, sliced
1 packet Sweet 'N Low

Brown chicken in large non-stick saucepan. Add remaining ingredients, except mushrooms and Sweet 'N Low. Cover and simmer 30 minutes. Add mushrooms and cook, uncovered, 10 to 15 minutes, or until chicken is tender. Stir in Sweet 'N Low.

PER SERVING (1/2 chicken breast):	Calories: 215	Protein: 31gm
Carbohydrate: 10gm	Fat: 4gm	Sodium: 565mg

Orange Herbed Chicken 4 servings

1 2 1/2-pound chicken,
   quartered and skinned
1 packet Butter Buds, made
   into liquid
1/4 cup frozen orange juice
   concentrate, undiluted

2 packets Sweet 'N Low
1 teaspoon oregano
1 teaspoon dry mustard

Place chicken in large skillet. In separate bowl, combine remaining ingredients and pour over chicken. Cover and simmer gently 20 minutes. Turn chicken and baste with sauce. Cover and simmer 15 to 20 minutes, or until chicken is tender. Transfer chicken to serving platter and pour sauce over chicken.

PER SERVING (1/4 chicken):	Calories: 215	Protein: 30gm
Carbohydrate: 9gm	Fat: 5gm	Sodium: 305mg

By using Butter Buds instead of butter in this recipe, you have saved 188 calories and 70 mg cholesterol per serving.

Chicken Cordon Bleu 4 servings

4 thin slices (about 2
   ounces) lean cooked ham
4 thin slices (about 2
   ounces) Swiss cheese
2 boneless, skinless whole
   chicken breasts (about 1
   pound), split and
   pounded thin

1/3 cup seasoned bread
   crumbs
1/4 teaspoon salt
1/8 teaspoon freshly ground
   pepper
1/8 teaspoon tarragon
   Dash garlic powder
1 packet Butter Buds,
   made into liquid

Preheat oven to 350°F. For each serving, place 1 slice ham and 1 slice cheese on chicken. Roll up and secure with wooden picks, if necessary. Combine bread crumbs and seasonings. Dip each chicken roll in Butter Buds, then in bread crumbs. Arrange in shallow baking dish; drizzle with remaining Butter Buds. Bake 40 minutes, or until chicken is tender.

PER SERVING (1 chicken roll):	Calories: 275	Protein: 35gm
Carbohydrate: 7gm	Fat: 10gm	Sodium: 675mg

By using Butter Buds instead of butter in this recipe, you have saved 188 calories and 70 mg cholesterol per serving.

Chicken Cacciatore

 2 servings

1 tablespoon vegetable oil
2 boneless, skinless chicken
    breasts (about 4 ounces
    each)
1/4 cup chopped onion
1/4 cup chopped green pepper
2 tablespoons diced celery
2 cloves garlic, minced
1/4 cup liquid Butter Buds

1/2 teaspoon oregano
1/2 teaspoon basil
2 medium-size ripe
    tomatoes, chopped
1/4 teaspoon rosemary
1/4 cup dry white wine
1/2 cup sliced mushrooms
Freshly ground pepper
    to taste

Heat oil in large skillet. Sauté chicken breasts about 5 minutes, or until golden brown on both sides. Transfer to platter. Add onion, green pepper, celery, and garlic to skillet and sauté until onion is transparent. Add Butter Buds, oregano, basil, tomatoes, and rosemary. Simmer, covered, until tomatoes are completely soft, 5 to 10 minutes. Return chicken breasts to skillet. Add wine and mushrooms. Season with pepper. Simmer, covered, about 20 minutes. Serve chicken breasts topped with tomato sauce. Serve over rice.

PER SERVING (1 chicken breast):	Calories: 305	Protein: 32gm
Carbohydrate: 16gm	Fat: 10gm	Sodium: 315mg

By using Butter Buds instead of vegetable oil in this recipe, you have saved 228 calories per serving.

Baked Chicken

 4 servings

1 packet Butter Buds
1/2 teaspoon paprika
1/2 teaspoon sage
1/2 teaspoon onion powder

Pepper to taste
1 2 1/2-pound broiler-fryer,
    cut up
1/2 cup dry white wine

Preheat oven to 375°F. In small bowl, combine Butter Buds and spices; rub over chicken, coating completely. Arrange in 13×9-inch pan. Pour wine over chicken. Bake about 50 minutes, or until tender and golden brown.

PER SERVING (1/4 chicken):	Calories: 210	Protein: 30gm
Carbohydrate: 2gm	Fat: 5gm	Sodium: 305mg

By using Butter Buds instead of butter in this recipe, you have saved 188 calories and 70 mg cholesterol per serving.

Buttery Skillet Chicken 4 servings

1 2 1/2- to 3-pound broiler-
fryer, cut up
1/4 cup all-purpose flour
1/4 cup vegetable oil

1/2 packet (4 teaspoons)
Butter Buds
Freshly ground pepper
to taste

Dredge chicken with flour. In small bowl, combine oil and Butter Buds. Mix well. In 12-inch skillet, over medium-high heat, heat oil mixture. When oil is hot, add chicken and cook until well browned on all sides, turning over frequently. Season chicken with pepper. Cover and heat on medium-low setting about 20 to 25 minutes, or until chicken is fork-tender. Uncover during the last few minutes.

PER SERVING (1/4 chicken):	Calories: 325	Protein: 30gm
Carbohydrate: 7gm	Fat: 18gm	Sodium: 195mg

By using Butter Buds instead of butter in this recipe, you have saved 94 calories and 35 mg cholesterol per serving.

Quick Chicken Stroganoff 3 servings

3 boneless, skinless chicken
breasts (12 ounces)
1 tablespoon vegetable oil
1/4 teaspoon salt
1/4 teaspoon sage
1 cup sliced fresh mushrooms
1 tablespoon chopped green
onion, including top

1/4 cup liquid Butter Buds
1/2 teaspoon thyme
1/8 teaspoon paprika
1 teaspoon cornstarch
2 tablespoons water
1/4 cup white wine
1/4 cup low-fat imitation
sour cream

Cut each chicken breast into strips, 1/2 inch wide and 1 1/2 to 2 inches long. Heat oil in large skillet; sprinkle chicken with salt and sage and add to skillet, turning often to brown on all sides. Add mushrooms, onion, Butter Buds, thyme, and paprika. Mix cornstarch with water. Add to skillet. Simmer 2 to 3 minutes, stirring constantly until sauce thickens. Stir in wine. Cook, covered, on low heat 3 minutes. Stir in sour cream, mixing thoroughly; do not boil. May be served plain or over noodles or rice or in toast cups.

PER SERVING (1 cup):	Calories: 240	Protein: 31gm
Carbohydrate: 5gm	Fat: 10gm	Sodium: 210mg

By using Butter Buds instead of butter in this recipe, you have saved 125 calories and 47 mg cholesterol per serving.

Tandoori Chicken

 4 servings

1 2 1/2- to 3-pound broiler-
fryer, cut up
1 teaspoon cayenne
1 teaspoon paprika
1/4 cup lemon juice
6 tablespoons red wine vinegar
3/4 cup chopped onions

1/4 cup chopped pimiento
3/4 cup plain low-fat yogurt
1 packet Butter Buds,
mixed with 1/4 cup
hot water
1/4 teaspoon ginger

Preheat oven to 375°F. Wash, dry, and skin chicken. Prick in several places with sharp knife point. Arrange chicken in glass baking dish. In separate bowl, mix cayenne and paprika with lemon juice and vinegar. Rub into chicken. Refrigerate 1 hour.

In blender container, combine onions, pimiento, yogurt, Butter Buds, and ginger. Cover and process at medium speed 10 seconds. Pour yogurt mixture over chicken. Bake 40 to 50 minutes, or until tender. Baste frequently with yogurt mixture while cooking.

PER SERVING (1/4 chicken):	Calories: 245	Protein: 36gm
Carbohydrate: 10gm	Fat: 6gm	Sodium: 350mg

By using Butter Buds instead of butter in this recipe, you have saved 188 calories and 70 mg cholesterol per serving.

Lemon Barbecued Chicken

 4 servings

1 2 1/2- to 3-pound broiler-
fryer, quartered
2 packets Butter Buds, made
into liquid
1/2 cup fresh lemon juice

2 teaspoons basil
2 teaspoons onion powder
1/2 teaspoon thyme
1/2 teaspoon garlic powder

Place chicken in shallow baking pan. In small bowl, combine remaining ingredients and mix until well blended. Pour sauce over chicken, cover tightly, and marinate in refrigerator 6 to 8 hours or overnight, turning chicken occasionally. Remove chicken from refrigerator about 1 hour before cooking. Cook 4 to 6 inches from broiler heat for about 20 to 25 minutes each side, brushing often with sauce.

PER SERVING (1/4 chicken):	Calories: 220	Protein: 33gm
Carbohydrate: 8gm	Fat: 5gm	Sodium: 530mg

By using Butter Buds instead of vegetable oil in this recipe, you have saved 456 calories per serving.

Sesame Chicken

 4 servings

1 cup crushed cheese-flavored crackers (approx. 84)
2 tablespoons sesame seeds
1 teaspoon basil
1 teaspoon thyme
1/2 teaspoon poultry seasoning
1/4 teaspoon garlic powder
1/8 teaspoon freshly ground pepper
4 boneless, skinless chicken breasts (about 1 1/4 pounds)
1 packet Butter Buds, made into liquid

Preheat oven to 375°F. In shallow baking dish, combine cracker crumbs, sesame seeds, and seasonings. Dip chicken breasts in Butter Buds, then roll in crumb mixture to coat well. Place in ungreased casserole. Drizzle with remaining Butter Buds. Bake, uncovered, 55 to 60 minutes, or until tender.

PER SERVING (1 chicken breast):	Calories: 325	Protein: 39gm
Carbohydrate: 16gm	Fat: 11gm	Sodium: 515mg

By using Butter Buds instead of butter in this recipe, you have saved 188 calories and 70 mg cholesterol per serving.

Cranberry Chicken

 4 servings

1/2 cup canned whole cranberry sauce
4 boneless, skinless chicken breasts, (about 1 pound) split and pounded thin
1/3 cup crushed bran cereal
3 tablespoons chopped nuts
1 packet Butter Buds, made into liquid

Preheat oven to 350°F. Place 1 tablespoon cranberry sauce on each chicken breast. Roll up and secure with wooden toothpicks. Combine bran cereal and nuts. Dip each chicken roll in Butter Buds, then coat with cereal mixture. Arrange chicken in oblong baking dish. Drizzle with all but 2 tablespoons remaining Butter Buds. Bake 40 to 45 minutes. In small saucepan, combine 2 tablespoons Butter Buds and remaining 1/4 cup cranberry sauce. Heat until smooth. Serve over chicken rolls.

PER SERVING (1 chicken roll):	Calories: 230	Protein: 23gm
Carbohydrate: 20gm	Fat: 6gm	Sodium: 280mg

By using Butter Buds instead of butter in this recipe, you have saved 188 calories and 70 mg cholesterol per serving.

Quick Chicken with Rice Parmesan

 4 servings

1 1/2 cups water
1 cup quick-cooking rice
2 cans (5 ounces each) boneless
  cooked chicken, diced, or
  about 1/2 to 3/4 pound
  diced cooked chicken

1 packet Butter Buds
1/3 cup grated Parmesan cheese

In covered saucepan, bring water to a boil. Add rice, chicken, and Butter Buds. Reduce heat to low and simmer 1 to 3 minutes. Remove from heat and let stand, covered, 8 to 10 minutes, or until rice is tender and all liquid is absorbed. Sprinkle with Parmesan cheese before serving.

PER SERVING (about 1 cup): Calories: 240	Protein: 20gm
Carbohydrate: 21gm Fat: 7gm	Sodium: 695mg

By using Butter Buds instead of butter in this recipe, you have saved 188 calories and 70 mg cholesterol per serving.

Easy Baked Chicken

 4 servings

1 2 1/2-pound broiler-fryer,
  cut up and skinned
3/4 cup tomato juice
1 packet Butter Buds, made
  into liquid
2 tablespoons red wine
  vinegar

1 tablespoon soy sauce
1 teaspoon ginger
1/2 teaspoon oregano
1 clove garlic, crushed

Arrange chicken pieces in baking dish. In separate bowl, combine remaining ingredients and pour over chicken. Cover and refrigerate several hours or overnight, turning chicken 2 or 3 times. Preheat oven to 375°F. Spoon marinade over chicken and bake, uncovered, about 1 hour, basting occasionally.

PER SERVING (1/4 chicken): Calories: 250	Protein: 39gm
Carbohydrate: 12gm Fat: 6gm	Sodium: 725mg

By using Butter Buds instead of butter in this recipe, you have saved 188 calories and 70 mg cholesterol per serving.

Vegetable-Chicken Dinner in Foil

 2 servings

1/2 pound fresh green beans, trimmed
1/2 pound diced cooked chicken
1/2 pound (2 medium-size)
    potatoes, pared,
    diced, and cooked

1 medium-size onion, sliced
1 packet Butter Buds

Steam beans 5 minutes, then combine with remaining ingredients in mixing bowl. Place chicken and vegetables on foil sheet, dull side out; pull up foil to cover and seal edges tightly by folding ends of foil over several times. Bake on grill, coals, or in preheated oven at 375°F 10 minutes, or until heated through.

PER SERVING (1 1/2 cups):	Calories: 290	Protein: 31gm
Carbohydrate: 31gm	Fat: 5gm	Sodium: 530mg

By using Butter Buds instead of butter in this recipe, you have saved 376 calories and 140 mg cholesterol per serving.

Tangy Barbecued Chicken

 4 servings

1/4 cup chopped onion
1 clove garlic, crushed
1 packet Butter Buds, made
    into liquid
1/2 cup catsup
1 tablespoon sugar

1 teaspoon distilled
    white vinegar
Dash cayenne
Dash chili powder
1 2 1/2 to 3-pound
    broiler-fryer, cut up

Cook onion and garlic in Butter Buds until soft. Add catsup, sugar, vinegar, cayenne, and chili powder. Simmer 5 minutes. Brush over chicken. Cook on preheated barbecue grill about 45 minutes, or until tender, turning once and basting often with sauce.

PER SERVING (1/4 chicken):	Calories: 255	Protein: 34gm
Carbohydrate: 16gm	Fat: 6gm	Sodium: 575mg

By using Butter Buds instead of vegetable oil in this recipe, you have saved 228 calories per serving.

Nice to know: 1 packet Sweet 'N Low can be substituted for the sugar in this recipe. You'll save 15 calories and 3 gm carbohydrates per serving.

Coq au Vin

 4 servings

1 2 1/2-pound broiler-fryer,
  cut up and skinned
1 1/4 cups tomato juice
  1/4 cup red wine vinegar
  1 chicken-flavor bouillon
    cube, crushed
  1 clove garlic, crushed
  1 packet Sweet 'N Low
1 1/2 cups small whole onions,
  peeled

2 cups (about 4 ounces)
  quartered fresh
  mushrooms
1 sprig parsley
1 bay leaf
1 teaspoon marjoram
1 teaspoon sage
1 teaspoon rosemary

Place chicken pieces in shallow baking dish. In separate bowl, combine tomato juice, vinegar, bouillon, garlic, and Sweet 'N Low. Pour over chicken. Allow to marinate, refrigerated, 3 to 4 hours.

Remove chicken and reserve marinade in small bowl. Preheat oven to 375°F. Brown chicken and onions in non-stick skillet. Return to baking dish. Add mushrooms. Tie herbs in cheesecloth and add to chicken. Pour marinade over all. Cover and bake 40 minutes. Baste with marinade sauce and continue baking, uncovered, 20 minutes, or until chicken is tender. Remove herbs before serving.

PER SERVING (1/4 chicken):	Calories: 225	Protein: 33gm
Carbohydrate: 11gm	Fat: 5gm	Sodium: 490mg

Note: If you don't own a non-stick skillet, you can spray your skillet with a non-stick coating agent.

Coq au Vin.

Herb-Basted Cornish Hens

 4 servings

2 cornish hens (about 1 1/2
  pounds each)
Freshly ground pepper
  to taste
Vegetable Stuffing (below)
2 packets Butter Buds

1/2 cup water
1/4 cup dry white wine
2 tablespoons fresh lemon
  juice
2 teaspoons tarragon
3 garlic cloves, minced

Preheat oven to 350°F. Season hens with pepper and stuff with Vegetable Stuffing. In separate bowl, combine remaining ingredients and pour over hens. Bake 1 1/2 hours or until tender, basting occasionally with sauce.

PER SERVING (1/2 cornish hen): Calories: 200	Protein: 19gm
Carbohydrate: 23gm Fat: 3gm	Sodium: 690mg

By using Butter Buds instead of butter in this recipe, you have saved 356 calories and 140 mg cholesterol per serving.

Vegetable Stuffing

 About 2 cups

1 packet Butter Buds
1/4 cup water
1/3 cup (about 1 medium-size)
  chopped carrot
1/3 cup (about 1 medium-size
  stalk) chopped celery

1/4 cup chopped onion
1 cup packaged herb-
  seasoned stuffing mix

Heat Butter Buds and water. Add carrot, celery, and onion and simmer 5 to 7 minutes. Add stuffing and mix well.

PER SERVING (about 1/2 cup): Calories: 75	Protein: 2gm
Carbohydrate: 16gm Fat: trace	Sodium: 240mg

By using Butter Buds instead of butter in this recipe, you have saved 88 calories and 35 mg cholesterol per serving.

Oven-Fried Fish Fillets 4 servings

1 pound white fish fillets
1/2 cup unseasoned croutons
    (approximately 3/8-inch
    cube)
1/4 cup chopped onion
2 tablespoons chopped green
    pepper

1 tablespoon chopped
    pimiento
1 teaspoon lemon juice
1 packet Butter Buds, made
    into liquid
1/4 teaspoon marjoram
1/4 teaspoon thyme

Preheat oven to 350°F. Split fillets into 4 serving portions approximately 4 ounces each. Combine croutons, onion, green pepper, pimiento, lemon juice, 1/4 cup Butter Buds, and seasonings. Arrange fillets in non-stick oblong baking dish and cover each with a portion of the crouton mixture, patting down firmly on the fish. Drizzle remaining Butter Buds over fillets. Bake about 15 to 20 minutes, or until fish flakes easily.

PER SERVING (one 1/4-pound fillet):	Calories: 205	Protein: 24gm
Carbohydrate: 5gm	Fat: 10gm	Sodium: 305mg

By using Butter Buds instead of butter in this recipe, you have saved 188 calories and 70 mg cholesterol per serving.

Note: If you don't own a non-stick baking dish, you can spray your baking dish with a non-stick coating agent.

Foil-Baked Fish 4 servings

4 fish fillets (1 pound)
1 cup (about 2 ounces) sliced
    fresh mushrooms
1 medium-size apple, sliced
1 packet Butter Buds, made
    into liquid

2 tablespoons sliced
    green onion
1/4 teaspoon thyme
1/8 teaspoon salt
1/8 teaspoon freshly ground
    pepper

Preheat oven to 350°F. On four separate pieces of aluminum foil, arrange 1 fish fillet with 1/4 cup mushrooms and a few apple slices. Combine Butter Buds, onion, thyme, salt, and pepper and pour over fish. Wrap up each serving tightly, sealing ends well. Bake about 15 to 20 minutes or until fish flakes easily.

PER SERVING (1 fillet):	Calories: 115	Protein: 17gm
Carbohydrate: 10gm	Fat: 1gm	Sodium: 365mg

By using Butter Buds instead of butter in this recipe, you have saved 188 calories and 70 mg cholesterol per serving.

Buttery Fish Roll-Ups 4 servings

1 pound white fish fillets
12 fresh or frozen asparagus
spears, each about 5-
inches long
1/2 cup water
2 tablespoons white wine

1 teaspoon chopped fresh
parsley
1/8 teaspoon thyme
Freshly ground pepper
to taste
1 packet Butter Buds
Paprika

Preheat oven to 350°F. Split fillets into 4 serving pieces. Cook asparagus spears in water until tender and crisp, about 5 minutes. Do not overcook. Reserve 1/4 cup liquid. In saucepan, combine asparagus liquid, wine, parsley, thyme, pepper, and Butter Buds. Heat on low until Butter Buds dissolve. Brush each fillet with sauce. For easier handling, split asparagus spears lengthwise. Depending on size of fillet, arrange 1 to 2 asparagus spears on top of each fillet. Roll fillet from thin to thick end. Secure with toothpicks. Place in lightly greased baking dish. Pour remaining sauce over fish rolls. Bake, covered, about 20 minutes. Remove from oven and preheat broiler. Uncover fish and baste with pan juices. Sprinkle fish lightly with paprika. Broil 2 or 3 minutes, or until golden brown. Remove toothpicks just before serving. Pour remaining pan juices over fish rolls.

PER SERVING (1 fish roll):	Calories: 105	Protein: 18gm
Carbohydrate: 3gm	Fat: trace	Sodium: 285mg

By using Butter Buds instead of butter in this recipe, you have saved 188 calories and 70 mg cholesterol per serving.

Bluefish Amandine

 4 servings

1/3 cup (1 1/2 ounces) slivered
  almonds
4 bluefish fillets (about
  1 1/2 pounds)
1 packet Butter Buds, made
  into liquid

1/2 teaspoon chopped fresh
  parsley
1/8 teaspoon freshly ground
  pepper
1/4 teaspoon almond extract
  (optional)

Preheat oven to 400°F. Arrange almonds in single layer on ungreased cookie sheet. Bake 3 to 4 minutes, or until golden brown. Set aside. Reduce oven to 350°F. Place fish in ungreased baking dish. Combine Butter Buds, parsley, pepper, and almond extract. Add almonds and pour mixture over fish. Bake, covered, 20 to 25 minutes, or until fish flakes easily.

PER SERVING (1 fillet):	Calories: 290	Protein: 37gm
Carbohydrate: 5gm	Fat: 11gm	Sodium: 340mg

By using Butter Buds instead of butter in this recipe, you have saved 188 calories and 70 mg cholesterol per serving.

Ginger Teriyaki Fish

 6 servings

2 pounds firm-fleshed fish,
  such as sea bass or
  snapper
1/2 cup chicken-flavor bouillon
  or stock
1/4 cup dry sherry
1 tablespoon soy sauce

1/2 teaspoon grated fresh
  gingerroot
2 teaspoons cornstarch
1 tablespoon water
1 packet Sweet 'N Low
1 tablespoon Dijon mustard

Preheat broiler. Spray rack over broiler pan with non-stick coating agent. Wipe fish with paper towel and place on broiler rack. In small saucepan, combine bouillon, sherry, soy sauce, and ginger; bring to simmering over moderate heat. Combine cornstarch with water and add to sauce. Stir until mixture thickens; remove from heat. Stir in Sweet 'N Low. Brush fish with 1/4 cup sauce. Broil 6 to 8 minutes, brushing fish twice with sauce. Fish is cooked when it flakes easily with a fork. Mix mustard with remaining sauce and serve over fish.

PER SERVING (5 ounces):	Calories: 170	Protein: 31gm
Carbohydrate: 3gm	Fat: 2gm	Sodium: 445mg

New England Style Clambake

 8 servings

8 ears sweet corn
8 baking potatoes
8 lobsters (1 1/2 pounds each)
48 hard-shell clams
2 bushels wet rock seaweed

4 packets Butter Buds,
    made into liquid
Freshly ground pepper
    to taste

About 4 to 5 hours before serving, dig a pit in the sand about 1 foot deep and 3 feet across and line bottom with smooth flat rocks. Build a wood fire on the rocks and keep it burning 1 1/2 to 2 1/2 hours, or until rocks are white hot.

Meanwhile, prepare food for steaming. Pull outer husks from corn and reserve. Pull inner husks back and remove silk. Replace inner husks. Scrub potatoes. Scrub lobsters and clams well to remove sand and excess dirt.

When stones are hot, quickly rake and shovel embers from pit. Line bottom of pit with 6 inches of seaweed. Layer potatoes, corn, lobsters, and clams alternately with seaweed. Top with reserved corn husks. Pour a pail of salt water over all. Cover food completely with a wet tarpaulin and anchor in place with large rocks. Steam food about 1 hour, or until vegetables are tender, lobster is pink, and clams are opened. Serve with Butter Buds and pepper.

PER SERVING (1 ear corn, 1 potato, 1 lobster, and 6 clams):		
	Calories: 440	Protein: 43gm
Carbohydrate: 58gm	Fat: 4gm	Sodium: 975mg

By using Butter Buds instead of butter in this recipe, you have saved 376 calories and 140 mg cholesterol per serving.

Tangy Barbecued Fish

 6 servings

1/2 cup unsweetened apple juice
    or cider
1/4 cup distilled white vinegar
1/4 cup sliced green onion,
    including tops
1 packet Butter Buds, mixed
    with 1/4 cup water
1 tablespoon bottled steak
    sauce

1 teaspoon salt
1 teaspoon tarragon
1/8 teaspoon freshly ground
    pepper
2 pounds fish steaks or
    fillets, 1-inch thick

In 1 1/2-quart saucepan, combine all ingredients except fish. Bring to a boil; reduce heat and simmer 20 minutes. Marinate fish in sauce at least 3 hours or overnight, turning pieces occasionally.

Prepare grill for barbecuing. If using a charcoal grill, position grilling rack 3 inches from coals. If an electric or gas grill is used, cook on medium setting. For easier handling, place fish in a large folding wire grill with long handles. Grill 10 to 12 minutes on each side, or until fish flakes easily with fork, basting every 5 minutes with sauce.

PER SERVING (one 5-ounce steak):	Calories: 125	Protein: 23gm
Carbohydrate: 6gm	Fat: 1 gm	Sodium: 620mg

By using Butter Buds instead of vegetable oil in this recipe, you have saved 152 calories per serving.

Nice to know: If a folding wire grill is not available, fish may be wrapped loosely in aluminum foil and cooked on the grill. Poke several holes in the foil with a fork to allow the smoke to penetrate and flavor the fish.

Sweet 'N Sour Shrimp 4 servings

1/4 cup thinly sliced onion
1 medium-size green pepper, seeded and cut into strips
2 teaspoons vegetable oil
1/4 cup rice vinegar
1 tablespoon soy sauce
2 teaspoons cornstarch

1/2 teaspoon ginger
1 can (8 ounces) juice-packed crushed pineapple
1 pound shrimp, cooked shelled, and deveined
6 packets Sweet 'N Low

In large non-stick skillet or wok, sauté onion and green pepper in oil until onion is transparent. In separate bowl, mix together vinegar, soy sauce, cornstarch, and ginger. Stir in pineapple and add to skillet. Stir over low heat until mixture thickens. Stir in shrimp and Sweet 'N Low. Heat thoroughly. Serve over hot cooked rice.

PER SERVING (1 1/4 cups):	Calories: 170	Protein: 23gm
Carbohydrate: 12gm	Fat: 3gm	Sodium: 496mg

Note: If you don't own a non-stick skillet you can spray your skillet with a non-stick coating agent.

Seafood Newburg

 4 servings

3 tablespoons all-purpose
flour
2 cups low-fat milk, divided
2 packets Butter Buds
1 teaspoon parsley flakes
1/4 teaspoon seafood seasoning

12 ounces cooked shrimp,
lobster, fish, or any
combination of above
(leftover baked fish
may be used)
4 slices enriched white
toast
Paprika

Mix flour with 1/2 cup milk. Stir to a smooth paste. Pour into top of double boiler and add remaining milk. Heat over boiling water until hot. Add Butter Buds and stir until smooth. Add parsley, seafood seasoning, and cooked seafood. Heat through. Serve over toast; sprinkle with paprika.

PER SERVING (1 cup):	Calories: 245	Protein: 25gm
Carbohydrate: 30gm	Fat: 2gm	Sodium: 595mg

By using Butter Buds instead of butter in this recipe, you have saved 376 calories and 140 mg cholesterol per serving.

Shrimp De Jonghe

 6 servings

2 pounds frozen shrimp, peeled
and deveined
1 1/2 packets Butter Buds, made
into liquid
1/2 cup dry sherry

2/3 cup seasoned bread
crumbs
1 clove garlic, minced
1 tablespoon dried parsley
flakes
1/8 teaspoon cayenne

Preheat oven to 375°F. Cook shrimp according to package directions. Arrange shrimp in 13×9-inch baking dish. In small bowl, combine Butter Buds and sherry; pour over shrimp. In separate bowl, mix together bread crumbs, garlic, parsley, and cayenne. Top shrimp with crumb mixture to cover. Bake about 20 minutes, or until heated through.

PER SERVING (1 cup):	Calories: 240	Protein: 38gm
Carbohydrate: 14gm	Fat: 2gm	Sodium: 560mg

By using Butter Buds instead of butter in this recipe, you have saved 188 calories and 70 mg cholesterol per serving.

Crab and Cheese Casserole

 6 servings

2 tablespoons vegetable oil
1 cup sliced celery
1/2 cup sliced onion
1/2 cup thinly sliced carrot
1/2 cup sliced mushrooms
1/4 cup diced green pepper
1 can (2 pounds) whole tomatoes
1 1/2 cups fresh or frozen
    flaked crab meat

1 cup cooked brown rice
1/4 teaspoon salt
1 packet Sweet 'N Low
1 bay leaf
1/2 cup (2 ounces) grated
    sharp Cheddar cheese

Preheat oven to 350°F. Heat oil in dutch oven or other oven-proof container. Sauté celery, onion, carrot, mushrooms, and green pepper until onion is transparent. Add remaining ingredients, except cheese. Let simmer 5 minutes. Remove bay leaf. Sprinkle with cheese. Bake 20 minutes.

PER SERVING (1 1/4 cups):	Calories: 185	Protein: 10gm
Carbohydrate: 17gm	Fat: 9gm	Sodium: 520mg

It's-A-Dilly Fish

 6 servings

1/2 cup low-fat imitation sour
    cream
2 tablespoons white wine
2 tablespoons fresh lime juice

1 packet Butter Buds
1 teaspoon dillweed
1 1/2 pounds fish fillets,
    about 1-inch thick

Combine all ingredients except fish and mix well. Pour over fish in oblong baking dish. Cover and refrigerate 3 or 4 hours. Cook fish in large folding wire grill on preheated barbecue grill about 10 minutes on each side, brushing several times with sauce.

PER SERVING (one 1/4-pound fillet): Calories: 110	Protein: 16gm
Carbohydrate: 2gm	Fat: 2gm	Sodium: 205mg

By using Butter Buds instead of vegetable oil in this recipe, you have saved 152 calories per serving.

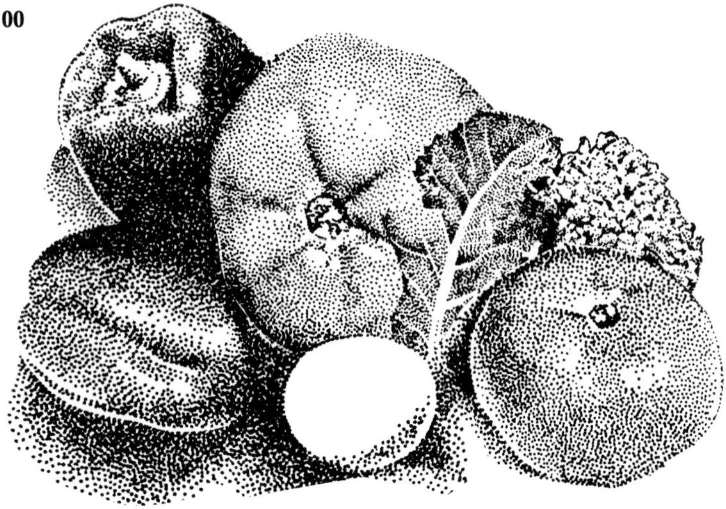

Lentil Loaf

N·S 4 servings

1 cup (6 ounces) dried lentils
2 1/2 cups water
2 bay leaves
2 large cloves garlic, minced
1 cup shredded carrots
1/4 cup chopped onion
1/4 cup chopped green pepper
1/4 cup chopped fresh parsley
1/4 cup toasted slivered almonds
1 egg, beaten
1 tablespoon lemon juice
1 packet Butter Buds
1/2 teaspoon basil
1/2 teaspoon oregano
1/2 teaspoon thyme
1/4 teaspoon freshly ground pepper
1/4 teaspoon dry mustard
3 tablespoons tomato paste
1/4 cup fine bread crumbs

Wash and drain lentils. Add to medium-size saucepan with water, bay leaves, and garlic. Bring to a boil. Cook, covered, until very tender, about 30 minutes; drain, reserving 1/4 cup liquid. Remove bay leaves. Preheat oven to 375°F. Transfer lentils to large mixing bowl. Add carrots, onion, green pepper, parsley, and almonds. Blend thoroughly. In separate bowl, combine egg, lemon juice, Butter Buds, reserved lentil liquid, and seasonings. Mix well. Add to lentil mixture. Blend in tomato paste and bread crumbs. Stir until all ingredients are thoroughly blended. Form into 6-inch loaf and place in shallow roasting pan. Bake, covered, 30 to 35 minutes. Uncover and bake 5 minutes longer.

PER SERVING (1 1/2-inch slice): Calories: 295 Protein: 17gm
Carbohydrate: 44gm Fat: 6gm Sodium: 320mg

By using Butter Buds instead of butter in this recipe, you have saved 188 calories and 70 mg cholesterol per serving.

Low-Calorie Manicotti 6 servings

12 manicotti shells
1 container (8 ounces) dry-curd
   cottage cheese
1 container (8 ounces) part-
   skim ricotta cheese
1 cup (about 4 ounces) grated
   mozzarella cheese
2 eggs

1/2 cup low-fat milk
2 packets Butter Buds
1/4 cup chopped fresh parsley
1 teaspoon oregano
1/2 teaspoon garlic powder
1/4 teaspoon white pepper
Tomato Sauce (below)

Preheat oven to 350°F. Prepare manicotti shells according to package directions. Drain. Cool quickly in cold water. In large bowl, combine cheeses, eggs, and milk and mix well. Blend in Butter Buds, parsley, oregano, garlic powder, and pepper. Stuff shells with cheese mixture. Coat bottom of baking dish with Tomato Sauce. Place filled manicotti shells on top of sauce. Cover shells with remaining sauce. Bake, covered, 40 to 45 minutes.

PER SERVING (2 shells):	Calories: 395	Protein: 26gm
Carbohydrate: 42gm	Fat: 13gm	Sodium: 660mg

By using Butter Buds instead of butter in this recipe, you have saved 250 calories and 93 mg cholesterol per serving.

Tomato Sauce About 4 cups

1 tablespoon vegetable oil
1/2 cup chopped green pepper
1/2 cup (1 medium-size)
   chopped onion
2 medium-size garlic cloves,
   minced
1 can (1 pound 12 ounces)
   peeled tomatoes,
   chopped

1/2 cup water
1 can (6 ounces) tomato paste
1/4 cup chopped fresh parsley
1 packet Butter Buds,
   made into liquid
1 teaspoon basil
1 teaspoon thyme
1/4 teaspoon freshly ground
   pepper

Heat oil in large saucepan or skillet. Add green pepper, onion, and garlic and sauté until tender. Add tomatoes, water, tomato paste, parsley, Butter Buds, basil, thyme, and pepper. Mix well. Simmer, covered, 25 to 30 minutes, stirring frequently.

PER SERVING (1/2 cup):	Calories: 70	Protein: 2gm
Carbohydrate: 10gm	Fat: 2gm	Sodium: 140mg

By using Butter Buds instead of vegetable oil in this recipe, you have saved 114 calories per serving.

Linguine al Pesto

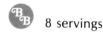 8 servings

1/2 cup (about 2 1/2 ounces)
    pignoli or pine nuts
2 1/2 cups fresh basil or
    2/3 cup dried basil
1 packet Butter Buds
2 tablespoons grated Parmesan
    cheese

1 tablespoon grated Romano
    cheese
1/4 teaspoon salt
2 cloves garlic, minced
2 tablespoons vegetable oil
1 pound uncooked linguine

Crush pignoli nuts with rolling pin. Combine with basil, Butter
Buds, cheeses, salt, and garlic in blender container. Cover and
process on medium speed about 10 seconds. Scrape down sides
of container and process 10 seconds longer. Add oil, 1
tablespoon at a time, processing 10 to 15 seconds after each
addition. Prepare linguine according to package directions;
drain. Toss pesto sauce with cooked noodles. Mix well.

| PER SERVING (1 cup): | Calories: 315 | Protein: 11gm |
| Carbohydrate: 48gm | Fat: 9gm | Sodium: 195mg |

*By using Butter Buds instead of butter in this recipe, you have
saved 94 calories and 35 mg cholesterol per serving.*

Vegetables

Buttery Corn on the Cob in the Husk (page 110) and baked potatoes are packed full of good nutrition and fiber. They can be low in calories, too, if they're drenched in Butter Buds instead of butter. Dress up your everyday vegetables creatively, without adding lots of calories, by using spices, herbs, and sauces made with Butter Buds and Sweet 'N Low. Take the salt shaker off the table, and if your doctor permits, spice up the flavor of vegetables with Nu-Salt, the perfect salt substitute.

Green Bean Casserole 8 servings

1 can (10 3/4 ounces) condensed
    cream of mushroom
    soup, undiluted
1/3 cup low-fat milk
1 packet Butter Buds
2 tablespoons fine bread
    crumbs
1/2 teaspoon paprika
    Freshly ground pepper
    to taste

1 pound (about 5 cups)
    green beans, trimmed
    and sliced in 1-inch pieces
2 medium-size green
    peppers seeded and sliced
4 small white onions,
    chopped
1 tablespoon grated
    Parmesan cheese

Preheat oven to 375°F. Combine soup, milk, and Butter Buds in medium-size saucepan. Heat until hot. In small bowl, combine bread crumbs, paprika, and pepper. Spray 1 1/2-quart casserole with non-stick coating agent. Alternate layers of vegetables, topping each layer with one-third of the mushroom sauce and 2 teaspoons of the bread crumb mixture. Top with grated cheese. Bake 1 hour.

PER SERVING (3/4 cup):	Calories: 85	Protein: 3gm
Carbohydrate: 11gm	Fat: 3gm	Sodium: 435mg

By using Butter Buds instead of butter in this recipe, you have saved 127 calories and 47 mg cholesterol per serving.

Artichoke Hearts Riviera 12 servings

2 packages (10 ounces each)
    frozen artichoke hearts
1/2 cup dry vermouth
1/4 cup liquid Butter Buds
1 tablespoon parsley flakes
2 teaspoons lemon juice

1 clove garlic, minced
1/2 teaspoon dry mustard
1/2 teaspoon tarragon
    Freshly ground black
    pepper to taste

Cook artichokes according to package directions. Drain well in colander. Combine remaining ingredients in saucepan. Cover and simmer about 5 minutes. Pour sauce over cooked artichoke hearts. Serve immediately.

PER SERVING (1 or 2 artichoke hearts):	Calories: 20	Protein: 1gm
Carbohydrate: 4gm	Fat: 0	Sodium: 60mg

By using Butter Buds instead of butter in this recipe, you have saved 63 calories and 23 mg cholesterol per serving.

Spinach Cheese Bake 6 servings

2 packages (10 ounces each)
  frozen chopped spinach,
  cooked and well drained
1 cup low-fat cottage cheese
1 packet Butter Buds, made
  into liquid
1/4 cup finely chopped onion
1/4 cup all-purpose flour
2 eggs, beaten

1/2 teaspoon salt
1/2 teaspoon Worcestershire
  sauce
1/4 teaspoon nutmeg
1/4 teaspoon freshly ground
  pepper
1/4 teaspoon thyme
1/4 cup grated Parmesan
  cheese

Preheat oven to 350°F. Combine all ingredients except
Parmesan cheese in 1 1/2-quart casserole. Sprinkle top with
Parmesan cheese. Bake, uncovered, 35 minutes, or until heated
through.

PER SERVING (3/4 cup):	Calories: 125	Protein: 11gm
Carbohydrate: 10gm	Fat: 3gm	Sodium: 595mg

*By using Butter Buds instead of butter in this recipe, you have
saved 125 calories and 47 mg cholesterol per serving.*

Gingered Carrots 6 servings

1 pound (8 or 9 medium-size)
  carrots
1/2 cup orange juice
2 tablespoons sugar
1 tablespoon cornstarch

1/2 teaspoon salt
1/4 teaspoon ground ginger
1 packet Butter Buds, made
  into liquid

Wash and peel carrots; slice diagonally about 1/2-inch thick.
Place in covered saucepan, with boiling, salted water; cook,
covered, until tender, about 15 minutes. In separate small pan,
combine remaining ingredients except Butter Buds. Heat until
mixture thickens and boils 1 minute; stir in Butter Buds. Pour
over drained hot carrots. Toss lightly to coat.

PER SERVING (1/2 cup):	Calories: 83	Protein: 1gm
Carbohydrate: 18gm	Fat: trace	Sodium: 375mg

*By using Butter Buds instead of butter in this recipe, you have
saved 125 calories and 47 mg cholesterol per serving. You can
also save 13 calories and 3 gm carbohydrate per serving by
substituting 3 packets Sweet 'N Low for sugar.*

Asparagus and Fresh Mushrooms

 4 servings

1/4 cup water
1/2 10-ounce package
    frozen cut asparagus
1 tablespoon vegetable oil
1/4 cup chopped onion
1/4 teaspoon rosemary
1/8 teaspoon white pepper

1 packet Butter Buds
1/2 teaspoon cornstarch
1/4 cup low-fat milk
1 cup (about 4 ounces)
    sliced fresh mushrooms
2 teaspoons lemon juice

Bring water to a boil in small saucepan. Add asparagus and simmer, covered, until asparagus is tender, about 6 to 8 minutes. Drain and set aside, reserving 1/3 cup liquid (add water if needed to make 1/3 cup). Heat oil in large skillet. Add onion, rosemary, and pepper. Sauté until onion is tender. Combine Butter Buds and reserved asparagus liquid; stir until dissolved. Add to skillet. Dissolve cornstarch in milk and add to skillet. Bring mixture to simmering and stir in asparagus, mushrooms, and lemon juice. Heat thoroughly.

PER SERVING (1/2 cup):	Calories: 70	Protein: 3gm
Carbohydrate: 6gm	Fat: 3gm	Sodium: 235mg

By using Butter Buds instead of butter in this recipe, you have saved 188 calories and 70 mg cholesterol per serving.

French Peas

 4 servings

1 package (10 ounces) frozen
    peas with onions
1 packet Butter Buds, made
    into liquid
1 cup (2 ounces) chopped
    lettuce leaves

1 tablespoon chopped
    fresh parsley
2 teaspoons tarragon
    Freshly ground pepper
    to taste
Paprika

Combine all ingredients except paprika, and cook, covered, over low heat 8 to 10 minutes, or until peas are tender. Sprinkle with paprika.

PER SERVING (1/2 cup):	Calories: 75	Protein: 5gm
Carbohydrate: 12gm	Fat: trace	Sodium: 330mg

By using Butter Buds instead of butter in this recipe, you have saved 188 calories and 70 mg cholesterol per serving.

Harvard Beets

 4 servings

1 can (1 pound) beets,
  sliced or diced
3 tablespoons red wine
  vinegar

2 tablespoons sugar
1 1/2 teaspoons cornstarch
1 packet Butter Buds

Drain beets, reserving 1/3 cup liquid. Combine vinegar, sugar, cornstarch, and reserved beet juice. Heat in saucepan on low heat. Add Butter Buds, stirring constantly. When sauce becomes thick and smooth, add beets and heat thoroughly. Transfer to serving dish.

PER SERVING (1/2 cup):	Calories: 70	Protein: 5gm
Carbohydrate: 15gm	Fat: trace	Sodium: 435mg

By using Butter Buds instead of vegetable oil in this recipe, you have saved 228 calories per serving.

Savory Tomatoes, Beans, and Squash

 6 servings

1 tablespoon vegetable oil
2/3 cup (4 ounces) chopped
  onions
1/4 cup chopped fresh parsley
1 teaspoon minced garlic
1 teaspoon basil
1 bay leaf
1/2 teaspoon tarragon
1/4 teaspoon sage
1/4 teaspoon thyme
1/4 teaspoon freshly ground
  pepper

1/4 teaspoon turmeric
1 packet Butter Buds,
  made into liquid
1 1/2 pounds (4 or 5 medium-
  size) tomatoes, sliced
  1/2-inch thick
1/2 pound fresh yellow
  squash, cubed (2 cups)
1/2 pound fresh green beans,
  cut into 1-inch lengths
  (2 1/2 cups)
1 tablespoon lemon juice

Heat oil in large skillet. Add onions, parsley, garlic, basil, bay leaf, tarragon, sage, thyme, pepper, and turmeric. Sauté 2 minutes. Add Butter Buds, tomatoes, squash, and green beans. Add water to half the depth of mixture. Mix well. Add lemon juice and simmer, covered, 20 to 25 minutes, or until beans are tender. Remove bay leaf.

PER SERVING (1 cup):	Calories: 80	Protein: 3gm
Carbohydrate: 11gm	Fat: 3gm	Sodium: 155mg

By using Butter Buds instead of butter in this recipe, you have saved 125 calories and 47 mg cholesterol per serving.

Baked Sweet 'N Sour Brussels Sprouts

 4 servings

1 package (10 ounces) frozen Brussels sprouts
1/3 cup liquid Butter Buds, divided
2 tablespoons cider vinegar
1 1/2 teaspoons sugar
1/4 teaspoon tarragon
1/8 teaspoon marjoram
1/8 teaspoon freshly ground pepper
1/3 cup sliced fresh mushrooms
1 tablespoon chopped pimiento

Preheat oven to 350°F. Cook Brussels sprouts in small amount of unsalted water just until thawed. Drain. Arrange sprouts in shallow baking dish. Combine 4 tablespoons Butter Buds, vinegar, sugar, tarragon, marjoram, and pepper in blender container. Cover and process on medium speed a few seconds. Pour over sprouts. Combine remaining Butter Buds, mushrooms, and pimiento. Sprinkle over sprouts. Bake, covered, about 15 minutes, or until sprouts are tender.

PER SERVING (2/3 cup):	Calories: 45	Protein: 3gm
Carbohydrate: 8gm	Fat: trace	Sodium: 160mg

By using Butter Buds instead of butter in this recipe, you have saved 125 calories and 70 mg cholesterol per serving. You can also substitute 1/2 packet Sweet 'N Low for the sugar in this recipe. You'll save 5 calories and 1 gm carbohydrate per serving.

Sweet 'N Sour Beets

4 servings

2 teaspoons cornstarch
1/2 cup water
1/4 cup distilled white vinegar
1 can (12 ounces) sliced or cubed beets, drained
2 packets Sweet 'N Low

In small saucepan, mix cornstarch with water and vinegar. Stir over medium heat until mixture thickens. Add beets and Sweet 'N Low. Let stand about 30 minutes. Just before serving, reheat until hot.

PER SERVING (1/3 cup):	Calories: 25	Protein: trace
Carbohydrate: 6gm	Fat: trace	Sodium: 100mg

Corn on the Cob in the Husk (page 110), Baked Sweet 'N Sour Brussels Sprouts, Stuffed Baked Potatoes (page 116).

Corn on the Cob in the Husk

 4 servings

4 ears unhusked corn
1 packet Butter Buds, made
into liquid

1/4 teaspoon garlic salt

Peel down corn husks enough to remove silk. Combine Butter Buds and garlic salt. Brush evenly over each ear of corn. Recover with husk. Heat 3 or 4 inches from coals or grill 20 to 30 minutes. Turn one-quarter the way around every 5 minutes. Remove husk and brush again with Butter Buds sauce. Serve remaining sauce with corn.

PER SERVING (1 ear of corn):	**Calories:** 82	**Protein:** 2gm
Carbohydrate: 17gm	**Fat:** 1gm	**Sodium:** 353mg

By using Butter Buds instead of butter in this recipe, you have saved 125 calories and 70 mg cholesterol per serving.

Cauliflower Polonaise

 6 servings

1 medium-size head
cauliflower
1 vegetable-flavor bouillon
cube
1 cup water
1/4 cup liquid Butter Buds
1 teaspoon all-purpose flour

1/8 teaspoon garlic powder
Freshly ground pepper
to taste
1 tablespoon chopped
fresh parsley
2 tablespoons coarse
bread crumbs

Bring small amount of unsalted water to a boil. Add cauliflower and return to boiling. Reduce heat and simmer, covered, just until tender, about 25 minutes. Drain. Place in serving dish and keep warm. Dissolve bouillon in water in saucepan. Bring to a simmer. Add Butter Buds, flour, garlic powder, and pepper. Heat, stirring constantly, until mixture is smooth and free of lumps. Pour sauce over cauliflower to coat. Lightly toss parsley with bread crumbs. Sprinkle half of mixture over cauliflower. Pour remaining sauce over cauliflower and sprinkle with remaining crumbs. Serve immediately.

PER SERVING (2/3 cup):	**Calories:** 55	**Protein:** 4gm
Carbohydrate: 10gm	**Fat:** trace	**Sodium:** 270mg

By using Butter Buds instead of butter in this recipe, you have saved 63 calories and 23 mg cholesterol per serving.

Creole Lima Beans

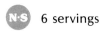 6 servings

3/4 cup (5 ounces) dried, small
    lima beans
3 cups water
2 bay leaves
1 tablespoon vegetable oil
1/2 cup (1 medium-size) chopped
    onion
1/2 cup (1 medium-size)
    chopped green pepper
1 teaspoon minced garlic
1/2 teaspoon dry mustard
1/2 teaspoon basil

1/4 teaspoon sage
1/4 teaspoon thyme
1/8 teaspoon freshly ground
    pepper
1/8 teaspoon marjoram
1 packet Butter Buds
1 teaspoon all-purpose
    flour
1 tablespoon wine vinegar
1 teaspoon lemon juice
1 1/2 cups (2 medium-size)
    diced ripe tomatoes

In saucepan, combine beans, water, and bay leaves. Bring to a boil and cook, covered, 2 minutes. Remove from heat and let stand 1 hour. Return to heat and simmer, covered, until tender, about 25 to 35 minutes. Drain, reserving liquid. Heat oil in large skillet. Add onion, green pepper, garlic, and seasonings. Saute until onion is tender. Add reserved bean liquid, Butter Buds, and flour. Stir to blend over low heat. Add vinegar, lemon juice, tomatoes, and lima beans. Simmer, uncovered, 7 to 10 minutes. Remove bay leaves.

PER SERVING (3/4 cup):	Calories: 130	Protein: 6gm
Carbohydrate: 20gm	Fat: 3gm	Sodium: 150mg

By using Butter Buds instead of butter in this recipe, you have saved 125 calories and 47 mg cholesterol per serving.

Carrots with Dill

2 servings

4 medium-size (about
    1/2 pound) carrots
1/4 cup liquid Butter Buds

1/2 teaspoon dillweed
Freshly ground pepper
    to taste

Peel carrots, then slice into 2-inch pieces. Boil in small amount of water until tender and crisp. Drain. Mix Butter Buds and dill in saucepan and heat on low. Add cooked carrots and heat thoroughly. Season with pepper.

PER SERVING (1/2 cup):	Calories: 60	Protein: 1gm
Carbohydrate: 12gm	Fat: trace	Sodium: 275mg

By using Butter Buds instead of butter in this recipe, you have saved 188 calories and 70 mg cholesterol per serving.

Broccoli with Yogurt

 6 servings

1 3/4 pounds fresh broccoli
1 1/2 cups plain low-fat yogurt
1 packet Butter Buds
1/4 teaspoon basil

1/8 teaspoon thyme
White pepper to taste
2 dashes marjoram
Paprika (optional)

Wash broccoli; discard larger leaves and cut off tough part of stalk. Cook, covered, in 1 inch boiling water 10 to 15 minutes, or until just tender. Drain and chill. Combine yogurt, Butter Buds, basil, thyme, pepper, and marjoram. Chill. Serve over chilled broccoli. Garnish with paprika.

PER SERVING (2/3 cup):	Calories: 75	Protein: 6gm
Carbohydrate: 10gm	Fat: 1gm	Sodium: 190mg

By using Butter Buds instead of butter in this recipe, you have saved 125 calories and 47 mg cholesterol per serving.

Pinto Bean Casserole

 4 servings

3/4 cup (about 5 ounces) dried
    pinto beans
1 quart cold water
1/2 teaspoon salt
1 clove garlic, pierced with
    a toothpick
1 bay leaf
4 ounces uncooked spinach
    noodles
1 tablespoon vegetable oil
1/2 cup diced celery

1/4 cup chopped onion
1/2 teaspoon basil
1/2 teaspoon dry mustard
1/2 teaspoon thyme
1/4 teaspoon sage
1 packet Butter Buds
1/4 cup chopped pimiento
Freshly ground pepper
    to taste
1/4 cup (1 ounce) grated
    mozzarella cheese

Pick over beans to remove any blemished ones. Wash in cold water. Drain. Soak in water overnight. Transfer beans and liquid to saucepan. Add salt, garlic, and bay leaf. Bring to a boil. Reduce heat and simmer, covered, until beans are tender, about 1 hour. Drain, reserving liquid from cooked beans. Cook noodles as directed on package. When tender, remove from heat, drain, and rinse noodles with cold water. Preheat oven to 350°F. Heat oil in large skillet. Add celery, onion, basil, mustard, thyme, and sage. Sauté until vegetables are tender, about 5 minutes. Measure 2 cups liquid from cooked beans. Add with

Butter Buds, pimiento, and pepper to celery-onion mixture in skillet. Mix thoroughly. Remove garlic and bay leaf. Add beans and noodles. Mix well. Transfer mixture to non-stick baking dish. Sprinkle top with cheese. Cover with foil. Bake about 30 minutes, or until cheese melts.

| PER SERVING (1 cup): | Calories: 285 | Protein: 12gm |
| Carbohydrate: 48gm | Fat: 5gm | Sodium: 250mg |

By using Butter Buds instead of butter in this recipe, you have saved 188 calories and 70 mg cholesterol per serving.

Note: If you don't own a non-stick baking dish, you can spray your loaf pan with a non-stick coating agent.

Baked Corn-Stuffed Tomatoes

 2 servings

2 medium-size ripe tomatoes
1 cup (1/2 10-ounce package)
    frozen kernel corn
1 tablespoon minced onion
1 tablespoon chopped green
    pepper
1 teaspoon vegetable oil

1/4 cup plus 2 teaspoons
    liquid Butter Buds
1/4 teaspoon thyme
1/4 teaspoon basil
    Freshly ground pepper
    to taste
1 tablespoon coarse bread
    crumbs

Preheat oven to 400°F. Cut the tops off tomatoes and scoop out seeds and pulp, leaving enough pulp to keep the tomato skin intact. Drain tomatoes upside down. Cook corn as directed on package. Saute onion and green pepper in oil until tender. Add corn, 1/4 cup Butter Buds, thyme, and basil. Season to taste with pepper. Heat gently 1 minute. Fill tomatoes with corn mixture. Combine bread crumbs and remaining 2 teaspoons Butter Buds. Place tomatoes in shallow baking dish and sprinkle tops with Butter Buds-crumb mixture. Bake 10 to 15 minutes, or until heated through.

| PER SERVING (1 tomato): | Calories: 165 | Protein: 6gm |
| Carbohydrate: 30gm | Fat: 3gm | Sodium: 235mg |

By using Butter Buds instead of butter in this recipe, you have saved 200 calories and 75 mg cholesterol per serving.

Marinated Peppers And Onions

 8 servings

3 medium-size green peppers,
    seeded and sliced
1 medium-size onion, thinly
    sliced
1 packet Butter Buds, made
    into liquid
1/3 cup distilled white vinegar

1 1/2 teaspoons salt
    2 cloves garlic, minced
1/4 teaspoon freshly
    ground pepper
2/3 cup water
    2 packets Sweet 'N Low

In 1 1/2-quart saucepan, combine all ingredients except Sweet 'N Low. Bring to boil and cook 3 minutes. Stir in Sweet 'N Low. Cool and refrigerate in tightly covered container.

PER SERVING (1/2 cup):	Calories: 30	Protein: 1gm
Carbohydrate: 7gm	Fat: trace	Sodium: 385mg

By using Butter Buds instead of vegetable oil in this recipe, you have saved 76 calories per serving.

Nice to know: This dish will keep in the refrigerator about 3 weeks.

Savory Vegetable Bake

 4 servings

1 package (10 ounces) frozen
    chopped broccoli
1 can (4 1/2 ounces) sliced
    mushrooms, drained
1/2 cup imitation sour cream
    dressing
1 packet Butter Buds
1/4 cup grated Parmesan cheese

1/2 teaspoon oregano
    Freshly ground pepper
    to taste
1 medium-size tomato,
    sliced
2 tablespoons seasoned
    bread crumbs

Cook broccoli just until tender; drain. Add mushrooms. Preheat oven to 325°F. In small bowl, combine sour cream dressing, Butter Buds, Parmesan cheese, oregano, and pepper. Mix with broccoli and mushrooms. Pour into 1-quart casserole. Top with sliced tomato. Sprinkle with bread crumbs. Bake 20 minutes, or until heated through.

PER SERVING (2/3 cup):	Calories: 95	Protein: 5gm
Carbohydrate: 8gm	Fat: 5gm	Sodium: 300mg

By using Butter Buds instead of butter in this recipe, you have saved 188 calories and 70 mg cholesterol per serving.

Oven-Braised Celery

 4 servings

6 medium-size stalks celery
1 chicken-flavor bouillon
  cube
2 tablespoons boiling water

1 clove garlic, crushed
1 packet Butter Buds,
  mixed with 1/4 cup
  water

Preheat oven to 375°F. Peel celery to remove strings. Slice diagonally into 1/2-inch-thick slices. Dissolve bouillon in boiling water. Combine with garlic and Butter Buds and mix thoroughly. Arrange celery in shallow baking dish. Pour sauce over top. Cover and bake 25 to 30 minutes, or until celery is tender.

PER SERVING (1/2 cup):	Calories: 25	Protein: 1gm
Carbohydrate: 4gm	Fat: trace	Sodium: 535mg

By using Butter Buds instead of butter in this recipe, you have saved 188 calories and 70 mg cholesterol per serving.

Foil-Baked Tomatoes

 4 servings

4 medium-size ripe
  tomatoes
1/4 cup seasoned bread crumbs

3 tablespoons grated
  Parmesan cheese
1 packet Butter Buds

Preheat barbecue grill or oven to 375°F. Cut out stems of tomatoes, leaving 1-inch cavity. Combine bread crumbs, cheese, and Butter Buds. Place each tomato on a piece of aluminum foil. Fill cavities of tomatoes with crumb mixture, sprinkling remaining crumbs over top. Cover tomatoes with foil, and seal ends tightly. Place on barbecue grill or in oven and cook about 20 minutes, or until tomatoes are cooked through.

PER SERVING (1 tomato):	Calories: 80	Protein: 4gm
Carbohydrate: 10gm	Fat: 1gm	Sodium: 300mg

By using Butter Buds instead of butter in this recipe, you have saved 188 calories and 70 mg cholesterol per serving.

Stuffed Baked Potatoes 2 servings

3 medium-size (about 1
pound) baking potatoes
3/4 cup low-fat milk
1 packet Butter Buds
1 slice reduced fat
cheese food

1/4 teaspoon marjoram
Freshly ground pepper
to taste
3 tablespoons liquid
Butter Buds
Paprika

Preheat oven to 400°F. Scrub potatoes and pierce several times with fork. Bake until tender, about 1 hour. Cut 1 potato in half and scoop out insides into bowl, discarding skin. Cut a thin slice off the tops of remaining potatoes and carefully scoop out insides, leaving about 1/2 inch of potato around inside of skin. Add scooped-out pulp to bowl with other potato pulp; reserve potato shells. Preheat broiler. Heat milk in top of double boiler. Add Butter Buds and stir until dissolved. Add cheese and marjoram, stirring constantly until cheese melts. Add hot liquid to potatoes. Beat until potatoes are light and free of lumps. (Add more milk if needed or desired for softer potatoes.) Add pepper. Spoon into potato shells, rounding tops. Brush tops with liquid Butter Buds and sprinkle with paprika. Broil until lightly browned.

PER SERVING (1 potato):	Calories: 260	Protein: 10gm
Carbohydrate: 50gm	Fat: 3gm	Sodium: 675mg

By using Butter Buds instead of butter in this recipe, you have saved 517 calories and 197 mg cholesterol per serving.

Red Cabbage with Diced Apples 6 servings

4 cups thinly sliced red
cabbage
1 green apple, peeled, cored
and diced
1/4 cup diced onion
2 tablespoons lemon juice

1 chicken-flavor bouillon
cube
1/8 teaspoon allspice
Dash pepper
3/4 cup water
2 packets Sweet 'N Low

Combine all ingredients except water and Sweet 'N Low in large saucepan. Add water. Cover and simmer 20 minutes, or until cabbage is tender. Stir in Sweet 'N Low.

PER SERVING (1/2 cup):	Calories: 35	Protein: 1gm
Carbohydrate: 8gm	Fat: trace	Sodium: 175mg

Mixed Vegetable Harvest 6 servings

4 ounces (2 cups) uncooked
thin egg noodles
1 packet Butter Buds, made
into liquid
1 tablespoon tomato paste
1 teaspoon basil
1 clove garlic, minced
1 teaspoon all-purpose
flour

1/3 cup low-fat milk
2 tablespoons white wine
Freshly ground pepper
to taste
1 package (10 ounces)
frozen mixed vegetables,
cooked and drained

Cook noodles according to package directions, omitting salt; drain. Rinse with cold water and set aside. In saucepan, combine Butter Buds, tomato paste, basil, and garlic. Dissolve flour in milk and add to Butter Buds mixture. Bring to a simmer. Reduce heat and add wine. Season with pepper. Simmer 2 or 3 minutes. Add vegetables to sauce and heat thoroughly.

PER SERVING (3/4 cup):	Calories: 125	Protein: 5gm
Carbohydrate: 23gm	Fat: 1gm	Sodium: 185mg

By using Butter Buds instead of butter in this recipe, you have saved 125 calories and 47 mg cholesterol per serving.

Whipped Potatoes à la Jardiniere 4 servings

3 cups pared, diced potatoes
1/3 cup low-fat milk
White pepper to taste
1 packet Butter Buds

1/2 cup finely chopped
cooked vegetables
(carrots, broccoli, etc.)

Cook potatoes in water until tender, about 15 minutes; drain. In medium-size saucepan, heat milk, pepper, and Butter Buds until hot but not boiling. Add milk mixture to potatoes. Beat until smooth and free of lumps. Fold in drained vegetables. Keep warm until served.

PER SERVING (2/3 cup):	Calories: 115	Protein: 4gm
Carbohydrate: 22gm	Fat: trace	Sodium: 240mg

By using Butter Buds instead of butter in this recipe, you have saved 188 calories and 70 mg cholesterol per serving.

Sweet Potato Soufflé 4 servings

1 can (8 ounces) sweet
potatoes
2 teaspoons bourbon (optional)
1/2 teaspoon salt
1/4 teaspoon nutmeg
1/8 teaspoon freshly ground
pepper

3 tablespoons all-purpose
flour
1 packet Butter Buds
1/2 cup low-fat milk
3 eggs, separated

Mash sweet potatoes with large fork. Season with bourbon, salt, nutmeg, and pepper. In small saucepan, dissolve flour and Butter Buds in milk. Heat just until mixture begins to thicken. Stir into sweet potatoes, blending well. Preheat oven to 325°F. Beat egg yolks until lemon colored. Slowly add to sweet potato mixture, stirring constantly. Beat egg whites until stiff. Gently fold into potato mixture. Turn into ungreased 1 1/2-quart soufflé dish. Bake about 1 1/4 hours, or until crust is firm and well-browned.

PER SERVING (2/3 cup):	Calories: 180	Protein: 8gm
Carbohydrate: 24gm	Fat: 5gm	Sodium: 580mg

By using Butter Buds instead of butter in this recipe, you have saved 188 calories and 70 mg cholesterol per serving.

Potatoes Anna 4 servings

1 1/2 pounds baking potatoes
1/4 cup chopped onion
3 tablespoons chopped fresh
parsley

Freshly ground pepper
to taste
1 packet Butter Buds
1/4 cup low-fat milk

Preheat oven to 375°F. Peel potatoes and slice very thin. Soak in ice water for about an hour; drain and dry with paper towels. Spray shallow baking dish with non-stick coating agent. Alternately layer potatoes, onion, parsley, and pepper. Combine Butter Buds with milk and heat in small saucepan until hot but not boiling. Pour over potatoes. Bake about 1 hour, or until potatoes are tender.

PER SERVING (2/3 cup):	Calories: 120	Protein: 3gm
Carbohydrate: 27gm	Fat: trace	Sodium: 235mg

By using Butter Buds instead of butter in this recipe, you have saved 188 calories and 70 mg cholesterol per serving.

Sautéed Potatoes

 4 servings

1 chicken-flavor bouillon
   cube
1 cup water
1/4 cup liquid Butter Buds
1/4 teaspoon garlic powder

1/4 teaspoon basil
1 teaspoon parsley flakes
2 medium-size (8 to
   10 ounces) baking
   potatoes

Combine bouillon and water in medium-size saucepan. Heat, stirring constantly, until bouillon dissolves. Add Butter Buds, garlic powder, basil, and parsley. Remove from heat, but keep warm. Peel potatoes and cut into 1/4-inch thick slices. Boil in lightly salted water until tender, about 15 minutes. Drain. Add potatoes to sauce and mix gently to coat.

PER SERVING (1/2 cup):	Calories: 70	Protein: 2gm
Carbohydrate: 15gm	Fat: trace	Sodium: 350mg

By using Butter Buds instead of butter in this recipe, you have saved 94 calories and 35 mg cholesterol per serving.

Brandied Sweet Potatoes

 8 servings

2 1/2 pounds sweet potatoes
1/4 cup liquid Butter Buds
1/4 cup brandy
1/3 cup raisins
2 tablespoons firmly packed
   light brown sugar
1/4 teaspoon mace

1/4 teaspoon ginger
1/4 teaspoon ground cloves
1 tablespoon grated
   orange peel
1/4 cup chopped fresh
   parsley

Preheat oven to 375°F. Peel and dice potatoes. Cook in unsalted water until tender, about 30 minutes. Drain. Mash with potato masher until free of lumps. In saucepan, combine Butter Buds, brandy, raisins, brown sugar, mace, ginger, and cloves. Heat gently until sugar melts. Using electric mixer, blend seasoned liquid into mashed potatoes. Add orange peel and parsley. Mix thoroughly. Transfer to 1 1/2-quart casserole sprayed with non-stick coating agent. Bake 30 to 40 minutes, or until top browns.

PER SERVING (1/2 cup):	Calories: 200	Protein: 2gm
Carbohydrate: 44gm	Fat: trace	Sodium: 72mg

By using Butter Buds instead of butter in this recipe, you have saved 47 calories and 18 mg cholesterol per serving.

Spinach Noodle Fettucine 4 servings

1 cup low-fat cottage cheese
1/2 cup plain low-fat yogurt
1/2 cup thinly sliced water
    chestnuts
1/2 cup toasted slivered
    almonds, divided
1/4 cup finely chopped pimiento
1 packet Butter Buds
1 tablespoon chopped fresh
    parsley

1 tablespoon grated
    Parmesan cheese
1/4 teaspoon oregano
1/4 teaspoon basil
1/4 teaspoon thyme
    Freshly ground pepper
    to taste
8 ounces (4 cups)
    uncooked spinach
    noodles

In medium-size bowl, blend cottage cheese into yogurt. Add remaining ingredients except noodles, using only 1/3 cup almonds. Mix well. Prepare noodles according to package directions, omitting salt. Drain. In a warm pan, toss hot noodles with cheese mixture. Turn onto warm serving platter and sprinkle with remaining almonds.

PER SERVING (1 1/4 cups):	Calories: 300	Protein: 14gm
Carbohydrate: 40gm	Fat: 9gm	Sodium: 295mg

By using Butter Buds instead of butter in this recipe, you have saved 188 calories and 70 mg cholesterol per serving.

Carrots Deluxe 6 servings

1 pound carrots, thinly sliced
1/2 cup chopped celery
1/4 cup diced onion
1/4 cup dry white wine

1 packet Butter Buds,
    mixed with 1/4 cup
    water
2 packets Sweet 'N Low

In medium-size saucepan, combine all ingredients except Sweet 'N Low. Cover and simmer 15 minutes. Stir in Sweet 'N Low. Simmer, uncovered, 5 minutes longer, or until tender.

PER SERVING (1/2 cup):	Calories: 55	Protein: 1gm
Carbohydrate: 10gm	Fat: trace	Sodium: 195mg

By using Butter Buds instead of butter in this recipe, you have saved 125 calories and 47 mg cholesterol per serving.

Spinach Noodle Fettucine.

Low-Calorie Vegetable Stuffing

 Approximately 8 cups

1 pound fresh mushrooms, sliced
3 cups (8 or 9 stalks) sliced, celery
2 cups (3 medium-size) peeled, cored, and chopped apples
1/2 pound finely shredded cabbage
1 cup (1 large) chopped onion
1/2 cup fresh bread crumbs
2 packets Butter Buds
1 teaspoon sage
  Freshly ground pepper to taste
2 egg whites, beaten

In large bowl, combine mushrooms, celery, apples, cabbage and onion. In separate bowl, combine bread crumbs, Butter Buds, sage, and pepper; toss to mix well. Stir into vegetables. Fold in beaten egg whites. Lightly stuff neck and body cavities of turkey. Tuck wing tips between the wing and body to prevent overcooking. Tie wings and legs to body with string to hold in place during cooking. Bake extra stuffing in small casserole, about 30 minutes, along with turkey.

PER SERVING (3/4 cup):	Calories: 60	Protein: 3gm
Carbohydrate: 12gm	Fat: trace	Sodium: 255mg

By using Butter Buds instead of butter in this recipe, you have saved 150 calories and 56 mg cholesterol per serving.

Baked Squash with Pecans

4 servings

2 acorn squash (1 pound each)
1/4 cup orange juice
1/4 cup chopped pecans
2 tablespoons diet margarine
4 packets Sweet 'N Low
1 teaspoon grated orange peel
1/2 teaspoon salt

Preheat oven to 350°F. Cut each squash in half. Scoop out seeds. Place cut side up in large baking dish and add water to fill dish 1/2 inch. Cover tightly and bake 35 minutes, or until tender. Preheat broiler. Scoop squash pulp out into bowl, leaving 1/4 inch around inside of shell. Combine remaining ingredients with pulp and beat with wooden spoon until light and fluffy. Spoon into shells. Broil until heated through and lightly browned, about 5 minutes.

PER SERVING (1/2 squash):	Calories: 180	Protein: 4gm
Carbohydrate: 25gm	Fat: 8gm	Sodium: 305mg

Sautéed Cabbage and Noodles

 4 servings

4 ounces (about 2 cups)
   uncooked whole-wheat
   noodles
2 1/2 cups water
2 cups shredded green cabbage
1 packet Butter Buds, made
   into liquid

1/4 teaspoon tarragon
1 tablespoon toasted sesame
   seeds
White pepper to taste

Boil noodles in water about 9 minutes, or until tender. Drain and rinse with cold water. In large non-stick skillet, saute cabbage in 5 tablespoons Butter Buds 5 minutes, or until cabbage is soft. Add tarragon, sesame seeds, and white pepper. Add noodles and remaining 3 tablespoons Butter Buds. Heat through. Serve immediately.

PER SERVING (3/4 cup):	Calories: 140	Protein: 4gm
Carbohydrate: 25gm	Fat: 2gm	Sodium: 230mg

By using Butter Buds instead of butter in this recipe, you have saved 188 calories and 70 mg cholesterol per serving.

Note: If you don't own a non-stick skillet, you can spray your skillet with a non-stick coating agent.

Poppy Seed Noodles

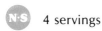 4 servings

6 ounces uncooked enriched
   egg noodles
2 packets Butter Buds, made
   into liquid

2 tablespoons minced onion
2 1/2 teaspoons poppy seeds
1/4 teaspoon onion powder

Prepare noodles according to package directions, omitting salt; drain. Combine 1/2 cup Butter Buds and onion in small saucepan. Cook over medium heat about 3 minutes, or just until onion is soft. Add cooked noodles, remaining Butter Buds, poppy seeds, and onion powder. Heat thoroughly.

PER SERVING (3/4 cup):	Calories: 195	Protein: 6gm
Carbohydrate: 37gm	Fat: 2gm	Sodium: 665mg

By using Butter Buds instead of butter in this recipe, you have saved 376 calories and 140 mg cholesterol per serving.

Wild Rice-Spinach Casserole

BB 6 servings

2 1/3 cups water
1/2 cup plus 2 tablespoons
    (5 ounces) uncooked long
    grain wild rice
1 tablespoon vegetable oil
1/3 cup chopped onion
1/3 cup chopped celery
1/4 cup chopped fresh parsley
3 tablespoons chopped pimiento
1/4 teaspoon garlic powder
1/8 teaspoon freshly ground
    pepper
1 package (10 ounces)
    frozen chopped spinach,
    thawed
2 tablespoons lemon juice
2 packets Butter Buds,
    made into liquid
1/3 cup chopped walnuts
1/2 teaspoon basil

Preheat oven to 425°F. In medium-size saucepan, bring water to boil. Add rice; reduce heat and simmer, covered, until all water is absorbed. Drain. Rinse rice with cold water. Set aside. Heat oil in large skillet. Add onion, celery, parsley, pimiento, garlic powder, and pepper; sauté about 5 minutes, or until onion is transparent. Add spinach, lemon juice, 1/2 cup Butter Buds, and rice; mix well and heat thoroughly. Remove from heat. In separate saucepan, combine walnuts and basil with remaining Butter Buds. Blend into spinach-rice mixture. Transfer to lightly greased 1 1/2-quart casserole. Bake, covered, about 20 to 25 minutes.

PER SERVING (3/4 cup):	Calories: 180	
Carbohydrate: 24gm	Fat: 7gm	Protein: 5gm
		Sodium: 355mg

By using Butter Buds instead of butter in this recipe, you have saved 250 calories and 94 mg cholesterol per serving.

Desserts

Just because you want to stay healthy and slim, you don't have to do without a superb selection of favorite desserts and baked goods. Imagine! Cookies, cakes, pies, and puddings, all reduced in calories because we've substituted Sweet 'N Low and Butter Buds. Plan an elegant affair with Quick Crêpes Suzette (page 143) or Bananas Foster (page 142). Looking for a quick but tasty and nutritious snack? How about Super Chocolate Chip Cookies (page 141) or Butter Buds Popcorn (page 143). Poached Pears in Blueberry Sauce (page 150) Apple Brown Betty (page 137) or old-fashioned Baked Apples (page 148) are a sumptuous way to end a great meal!

Whole-Wheat Banana Spice Cake

 18 servings

1 1/2 cups sifted whole-wheat flour
1 1/2 cups sugar
1 cup sifted all-purpose flour
1 1/2 teaspoons cinnamon
1 1/4 teaspoons baking powder
1 1/4 teaspoons baking soda
3/4 teaspoon nutmeg

1/2 teaspoon salt
1/2 teaspoon ground cloves
1 packet Butter Buds, made into liquid
2/3 cup buttermilk
1 1/4 cups mashed ripe bananas
2 eggs
2 cups Delicious Whipped Topping (page 128)

Preheat oven to 350°F. Spray 13×9-inch baking pan with non-stick coating agent. Combine dry ingredients in medium-size bowl. In separate bowl, combine Butter Buds, buttermilk, bananas, and eggs. Beat at low speed with electric mixer 1 minute. Gradually add dry ingredients and beat until well blended. Pour batter into prepared pan. Bake 35 to 40 minutes, or until toothpick inserted in center comes out clean. Transfer pan to cooling rack. When fully cooled, spread with Delicious Whipped Topping.

PER SERVING (one 3×2-inch piece):	Calories: 165	Protein: 4gm
Carbohydrate: 34gm	Fat: 2gm	Sodium: 240mg

By using Butter Buds instead of butter in this recipe, you have saved 42 calories and 16 mg cholesterol per serving.

Note: There's no need to spray with non-stick coating agent if you own a non-stick 13×9-inch baking pan.

Holiday Cherry Cake

 About 8 servings

1 cup sifted all-purpose flour
1 teaspoon baking soda
1 teaspoon cinnamon
1/4 teaspoon baking powder
1/4 teaspoon salt
1/4 teaspoon allspice
2 eggs
1/4 cup sugar
8 packets Sweet 'N Low
1 packet Butter Buds, mixed with 1/4 cup water

1 teaspoon vanilla
1/4 teaspoon almond extract
1/2 cup canned unsweetened cherries, pitted and cut in half
1 cup shredded, unpeeled raw zucchini (2 small)
1/2 cup thinly sliced almonds

Preheat oven to 350°F. Spray 9×5-inch loaf pan with non-stick coating agent. In medium-size bowl, sift together flour, baking soda, cinnamon, baking powder, salt, and allspice. In separate bowl, beat eggs with electric mixer, until light and fluffy. Gradually beat in sugar, Sweet 'N Low, Butter Buds, vanilla, and almond extract. Toss cherries with flour to coat. Fold sugar mixture into creamed mixture. Stir in cherries, zucchini, and almonds. Mix just to blend. Pour into prepared pan; bake 40 to 45 minutes, or until toothpick inserted in center comes out clean. Let stand 5 minutes, then turn out onto cooling rack until fully cool.

PER SERVING (one 1-inch slice):	Calories: 165	Protein: 5gm
Carbohydrate: 23gm	Fat: 6gm	Sodium: 340mg

By using Butter Buds instead of butter in this recipe, you have saved 94 calories and 35 mg cholesterol per serving.

Note: There's no need to spray with a non-stick coating agent if you own a non-stick 9×5-inch loaf pan.

Quick Tea Cake

 12 servings

2 cups sifted all-purpose
   flour
1/4 cup sugar
6 packets Sweet 'N Low
1 tablespoon baking powder
1/4 teaspoon salt

1/3 cup diet margarine
1 egg
3/4 cup buttermilk
1 teaspoon vanilla
1 cup finely chopped
   pecans

Preheat oven to 375°F. Spray 9-inch layer pan with non-stick coating agent. In medium-size bowl, sift flour, sugar, Sweet 'N Low, baking powder, and salt several times. Cut in margarine with pastry blender or knife until mixture resembles cornmeal. Beat egg until thick and lemon colored; add buttermilk and vanilla. Add gradually to dry ingredients. Stir in pecans. Pour batter into prepared pan. Bake about 25 to 30 minutes. Let stand 10 minutes, then turn out onto cooling rack.

PER SERVING (1/12 of cake):	Calories: 190	Protein: 4gm
Carbohydrate: 20gm	Fat: 10gm	Sodium: 175mg

Note: There's no need to spray with a non-stick coating agent if you own a non-stick 9-inch layer pan.

Blow-Away Sponge Cake

 12 servings

1/2 cup cornstarch
2 tablespoons all-purpose flour
1 teaspoon baking powder
3 eggs
1/3 cup sugar

4 packets Sweet 'N Low
2 cups Delicious Whipped Topping (below)
12 medium-size fresh strawberries

Preheat oven to 375°F. Spray two 8-inch round layer pans with non-stick coating agent. Sift together cornstarch, flour, and baking powder. In separate deep bowl, beat eggs with electric mixer until foamy. Beat in sugar and Sweet 'N Low gradually, and continue beating 5 minutes or until mixture is very thick and lemon colored. Gently fold in dry ingredients, a few tablespoons at a time, mixing carefully and thoroughly. Turn mixture into prepared pans. Place in oven and reduce heat to 350°F. Bake 15 minutes, or until cake begins to shrink from sides of pan and top springs back when lightly pressed with finger. Let stand 1 or 2 minutes. Loosen sides and turn onto cooling rack. When cool, fill and frost with Delicious Whipped Topping. Top with strawberries.

PER SERVING (1/12 of cake):	Calories: 85		Protein: 3gm
Carbohydrate: 15gm		Fat: 2gm	Sodium: 50mg

Note: There's no need to spray with a non-stick coating agent if you own non-stick 8-inch layer pans.

Delicious Whipped Topping

About 1 cup

3 tablespoons plain low-fat yogurt
3/4 cup part-skim ricotta cheese

1 teaspoon vanilla
2 packets Sweet 'N Low

In small deep bowl, beat yogurt and ricotta cheese with electric mixer until smooth and creamy. Add vanilla and Sweet 'N Low and continue beating until mixture is thoroughly blended. Mixture will keep in refrigerator several days. Rewhip before serving. Serve as frosting on cakes and as topping on pies or fruit desserts.

PER SERVING (2 tablespoons):	Calories: 18		Protein: 1gm
Carbohydrate: 1gm		Fat: 1gm	Sodium: 16mg

Banana Cream Pie

 8 servings

1 envelope unflavored gelatin
1/2 cup evaporated skim milk
3 eggs
1 cup low-fat milk
6 packets Sweet 'N Low
2 teaspoons vanilla

2 medium-size bananas,
peeled and sliced
1 tablespoon fresh lemon
juice
1 9-inch Cracker Crumb
Crust (below)

In top of double boiler, soften gelatin in evaporated milk. In medium-size bowl, beat eggs and low-fat milk until frothy; add to double boiler. Heat over hot water, stirring constantly, until mixture coats a metal spoon. Remove from heat. Stir in Sweet 'N Low and vanilla. Toss banana slices in lemon juice and arrange on bottom of prepared pie crust. Pour filling over bananas. Refrigerate several hours, until set.

PER SERVING (1/8 of pie):	Calories: 191	Protein: 7gm
Carbohydrate: 32gm	Fat: 4gm	Sodium: 217mg

Cracker Crumb Crust

 One 9-inch crust

6 graham crackers (2 1/2-
inch squares), crushed
6 rectangular melba toast
crackers, crushed
(about 1/2 cup)

1 tablespoon sugar
1 teaspoon cinnamon
1/4 cup liquid Butter Buds

Spray 9-inch pie dish with non-stick coating agent. Combine graham cracker and melba toast crumbs, sugar, and cinnamon in mixing bowl. Gradually add Butter Buds, 1 tablespoon at a time, mixing well after each addition. Press into bottom and up sides of pie dish. Refrigerate until ready to use.

PER SERVING (1/8 of crust):	Calories: 74	Protein: 2gm
Carbohydrate: 14gm	Fat: 2gm	Sodium: 152mg

By using Butter Buds instead of butter in this recipe, you have saved 47 calories and 18 mg cholesterol per serving. If you substitute 1 packet Sweet 'N Low for the sugar in this recipe, you'll save 5 calories and 1 gram carbohydrate per serving.

Note: There's no need to spray with a non-stick coating agent if you own a non-stick 9-inch pie dish.

Cheesecake

 8 servings

2 envelopes unflavored gelatin
1/4 cup sugar, divided
1/4 teaspoon salt
2 packets Butter Buds, divided
1/2 cup plus 3 tablespoons
    unsweetened pineapple
    juice, divided
1 cup low-fat milk
2 eggs, separated
1 container (8 ounces) dry-
    curd cottage cheese

1/2 cup juice packed
    crushed pineapple,
    drained
1 tablespoon grated lemon
    peel
1/2 cup graham cracker
    crumbs
1 teaspoon vanilla
1 tablespoon lemon juice

Mix gelatin, 3 tablespoons sugar, salt, 1 packet Butter Buds, 1/2 cup pineapple juice, milk, and egg yolks in top of double boiler. Place over boiling water and cook, stirring constantly, until gelatin dissolves and mixture thickens slightly. Cool.

In medium-size bowl, beat cottage cheese until smooth. (Use a potato masher for best results.) Beat in crushed pineapple and lemon peel. Add cooled gelatin mixture. In separate small bowl, combine graham cracker crumbs, remaining packet Butter Buds and vanilla. Add remaining pineapple juice and lemon juice. Mix well. Stir into cheese mixture. In separate bowl, beat egg whites until they hold their shape. Gradually add remaining sugar and beat until stiff. Fold into cheese-crumb mixture. Pour into 9-inch pie plate. Chill until firm.

PER SERVING (1/8 of cake):	Calories: 125	Protein: 10gm
Carbohydrate: 15gm	Fat: 2gm	Sodium: 360mg

By using Butter Buds instead of butter in this recipe, you have saved 188 calories and 70 mg cholesterol per serving. You can also substitute 6 packets Sweet 'N Low for the sugar in this recipe and save 20 calories and 5 gm carbohydrates per serving.

Chocolate Mousse (page 132), Cheesecake, Cherry Dumplings (page 132).

Cherry Dumplings

 4 servings

1 can (1 pound) pitted,
   water-packed tart red
   cherries, undrained
3 tablespoons sugar
1 packet Butter Buds
3/4 teaspoon cornstarch

3/4 cup sifted cake flour
3/4 teaspoon baking powder
1/8 teaspoon salt
1 tablespoon grated
   orange peel
1 tablespoon low-fat milk

Preheat oven to 350°F. In saucepan, combine cherries with juice, sugar, Butter Buds, and cornstarch. Bring to a boil. Remove from heat and transfer to 1-quart baking dish. In small bowl, mix flour, baking powder, and salt. Add orange peel, milk, and 3 tablespoons hot cherry sauce. Mix lightly until moist. Drop tablespoonfuls into cherry sauce to make 4 dumplings. Cover and bake about 20 minutes, or until dumplings become light and cherries bubble. Serve warm.

PER SERVING (1 dumpling with sauce):	Calories: 165	Protein: 2gm
Carbohydrate: 35gm	Fat: trace	Sodium: 350mg

By using Butter Buds instead of butter in this recipe, you have saved 188 calories and 70 mg cholesterol per serving. You can also substitute 4 packets Sweet 'N Low for the sugar in this recipe and save 30 calories and 8 gm carbohydrates per serving.

Chocolate Mousse

 8 servings

1 envelope unflavored gelatin
2 tablespoons unsweetened
   cocoa
2 eggs, separated

2 cups low-fat milk
   divided
5 packets Sweet 'N Low
1 1/2 teaspoons vanilla

In medium-size saucepan, mix gelatin and cocoa. In separate bowl, beat egg yolks with 1 cup milk. Blend into gelatin mixture. Let stand 1 minute to soften gelatin. Stir over low heat until gelatin is completely dissolved, about 5 minutes. Add remaining milk, Sweet 'N Low, and vanilla. Pour into large bowl and chill, stirring occasionally, until mixture mounds slightly when dropped from spoon. In separate large bowl, beat egg whites until soft peaks form; gradually add gelatin mixture and beat until doubled in volume, about 5 minutes. Chill until mixture is slightly thickened. Turn into dessert dishes or 1-quart bowl and chill until set.

PER SERVING (1/2 cup):	Calories: 65	Protein: 5gm
Carbohydrate: 5gm	Fat: 3gm	Sodium: 65mg

Pumpkin Pie

 8 servings

1 cup (1/2 1-pound can)
  pumpkin
1 egg, beaten
4 packets Sweet 'N Low
1/2 teaspoon cinnamon
1/4 teaspoon salt

1/8 teaspoon ground cloves
1 cup low-fat milk,
  scalded
1 9-inch Cracker Crumb
  Crust (page 129)

Preheat oven to 325°F. In medium-size bowl, combine all ingredients except milk and pie crust. Gradually add milk; stir to mix thoroughly. Pour into prepared pie crust. Bake 1 hour, or until knife inserted in center comes out clean. Serve warm or chilled.

PER SERVING (1/8 of pie):	Calories: 85	Protein: 3gm
Carbohydrate: 14gm	Fat: 2gm	Sodium: 175mg

Lemon Chiffon Pie

 8 servings

1 envelope unflavored gelatin
3/4 cup sugar, divided
1/2 cup water
1/4 cup lemon juice
2 eggs, separated
1 packet Butter Buds

1 teaspoon grated lemon
  peel
1 8-inch Low-Sodium Pie
  Crust (page 134)
Lemon slices

In top of double boiler, combine gelatin and 1/2 cup sugar. Beat in water, lemon juice, and egg yolks. Heat, stirring constantly, until hot. Remove 1/2 cup of hot mixture to small bowl and slowly beat in Butter Buds, mixing well. Put Butter Buds mixture back into double boiler. Cook, stirring constantly, until mixture thickens and coats a metal spoon. Remove from heat and add lemon peel. Cool slightly. Chill until thickened but not firm.

Beat egg whites until foamy; gradually add remaining sugar, beating until stiff. Fold egg whites into chilled gelatin mixture. Pour into 8-inch pie crust. Garnish with lemon slices. Chill several hours, until firm.

PER SERVING (1/8 of pie):	Calories: 115	Protein: 2gm
Carbohydrate: 22gm	Fat: 2gm	Sodium: 140mg

By using Butter Buds instead of butter in this recipe, you have saved 94 calories and 35 mg cholesterol per serving.

Low-Sodium Pie Crust 8 servings

1 cup sifted all-purpose flour
1 packet Butter Buds
1/4 teaspoon cinnamon
1/8 teaspoon mace

1 teaspoon sesame seeds
2 tablespoons plus 1
    teaspoon vegetable oil
2 to 3 tablespoons ice water

Blend flour with Butter Buds, cinnamon, mace, and sesame seeds. Add oil gradually, mixing into flour with a fork. When all of the oil has been added, work mixture lightly between fingertips until mixture is the size of small peas. Gradually add just enough ice water until dough is moist enough to hold together. Do not overwork dough. Form into a ball and roll out on floured surface with floured rolling pin, to a circle 1 inch larger than inverted 8- or 9-inch pie pan. Carefully transfer pastry to pie plate. Press dough into bottom and sides of pan, gently patting out air pockets. Preheat oven to 450°F. Prick bottom and sides of pastry with fork. Bake 8 to 10 minutes, or until lightly golden brown. Cool before using.

PER SERVING (1/8 of crust):	Calories: 95	Protein: 1gm
Carbohydrate: 11gm	Fat: 4gm	Sodium: 110mg

By using Butter Buds instead of butter in this recipe, you have saved 94 calories and 35 mg cholesterol per serving.

Apple Delight 6 servings

2 tablespoons margarine,
    chilled
1/3 cup sifted all-purpose
    flour
3/4 cup part-skim ricotta
    cheese

6 medium-size (about 2
    pounds) apples, peeled,
    cored, and finely sliced
1 tablespoon lemon juice
1/2 teaspoon cinnamon
2 packets Sweet 'N Low

Cut margarine into flour with pastry blender or fork and mix with fingertips until mixture resembles coarse oatmeal. Stir in ricotta cheese and mix into a ball. Wrap in waxed paper and refrigerate at least 2 hours before rolling.

Preheat oven to 375°F. In large bowl, toss apples with lemon juice, cinnamon, and Sweet 'N Low. Arrange in 8- or 9-inch pie plate. On lightly floured surface, with floured rolling pin, carefully roll out pastry to fit over top of pie plate. Lift over apples; press and shape to fit edge of pie plate. Imprint edges with tip of floured teaspoon. Bake 40 to 45 minutes, or until crust is golden brown and apples are tender. Serve warm or chilled.

PER SERVING (1/6 of pie):	Calories: 190	Protein: 5gm
Carbohydrate: 33gm	Fat: 8gm	Sodium: 90mg

Single Crust Pastry Shell

 8 servings

1 cup all-purpose flour
1/4 teaspoon salt
2 tablespoons plus 2
  teaspoons vegetable
  shortening

2 tablespoons plus 2
  teaspoons liquid
  Butter Buds
1 tablespoon cold water

In mixing bowl, combine flour and salt. Cut in shortening, using a pastry blender or two knives, until mixture is the size of small peas. Add Butter Buds and mix lightly with fork. Add water, 1 teaspoon at a time, until dough is just moist enough to hold together. Form a ball. On floured surface, with floured rolling pin, roll dough out to a circle 1 inch larger than inverted 8- or 9-inch pie pan. Fold pastry in half and transfer to pie pan; unfold and fit loosely into pan, gently patting out any air pockets.

Unbaked pastry shell: Prepare single crust as directed. Fold edges to form a standing rim; flute. Pour in filling and bake as directed in recipe.

Baked pastry shell: Preheat oven to 450°F. Prepare as directed for unbaked pastry shell. Prick bottom and sides with fork. Bake 8 to 10 minutes, or until lightly golden brown. Cool.

PER SERVING (1/8 pie shell):	Calories: 95	Protein: 2gm
Carbohydrate: 12gm	Fat: 4gm	Sodium: 105mg

By using Butter Buds instead of butter in this recipe, you have saved 62 calories and 23 mg cholesterol per serving.

Sweetheart Cupcakes

 24 cupcakes

1 package (18 1/2 ounces)
    butter recipe cake mix
2 packets Butter Buds, made
    into liquid
3 eggs
1/4 cup water

Fluffy Pink Frosting
    (below)
Cinnamon or heart-
    shaped candies
    (optional)

Preheat oven to 325°F. Place paper liners in cupcake tins. Combine cake mix, Butter Buds, eggs, and water in large mixing bowl; beat at low speed until moistened, about 1 minute. Beat 2 minutes at high speed. Fill cupcake tins 2/3 full. Bake 20 to 25 minutes, or until lightly browned and center springs back when touched lightly. Frost when fully cool. Decorate with candies.

PER SERVING (1 frosted cupcake): Calories: 115	Protein: 2gm
Carbohydrate: 20gm Fat: 3gm	Sodium: 185mg

By using Butter Buds instead of butter in this recipe, you have saved 30 calories and 12 mg cholesterol per serving.

Fluffy Pink Frosting

 About 1 1/2 cups

1/4 cup sugar
1 tablespoon water
1 packet Sweet 'N Low
1 egg white

1/8 teaspoon cream of tartar
1/4 teaspoon vanilla
2 drops red food coloring

In top of double boiler, combine sugar, water, Sweet 'N Low, egg white, and cream of tartar. Using an electric mixer, beat on high speed 1 minute. Set over boiling water and beat until mixture forms soft peaks, about 4 minutes. Remove from heat and add vanilla and food coloring. Continue beating 1 minute, or until thick enough to spread.

PER SERVING (1 tablespoon): Calories: 10	Protein: trace
Carbohydrate: 2gm Fat: 0	Sodium: trace

Apple Brown Betty

 4 servings

1 cup lightly packed soft
   bread crumbs
1/4 cup firmly packed light
   brown sugar
1 teaspoon cinnamon
1 packet Butter Buds, mixed
   with 1/4 cup water

3 large baking apples,
   peeled, cored, and
   sliced
2 tablespoons granulated
   sugar
2 tablespoons fresh lemon
   juice

Preheat oven to 375°F. In small bowl, toss bread crumbs with brown sugar, cinnamon, and Butter Buds. In 1-quart casserole, combine apples, granulated sugar, lemon juice, and 3/4 cup crumb mixture. Press mixture down lightly. Sprinkle with remaining crumbs. Bake 45 minutes, or until apples are tender and top is browned.

PER SERVING (2/3 cup):	Calories: 210	Protein: 1gm
Carbohydrate: 49gm	Fat: 1gm	Sodium: 285mg

By using Butter Buds instead of butter in this recipe, you have saved 188 calories and 70 mg cholesterol per serving.

Chocolate Crinkles

 4 dozen cookies

2 cups sifted all-purpose
   flour
2 teaspoons baking powder
1 cup sugar
1/4 cup vegetable oil
1 packet Butter Buds, mixed
   with 1/4 cup hot water

4 ounces unsweetened
   baking chocolate,
   melted and cooled
2 teaspoons vanilla
3 eggs

Sift together flour and baking powder; set aside. In separate bowl, combine sugar, oil, Butter Buds, chocolate, and vanilla. Beat in eggs. Add dry ingredients and beat until well blended. Cover; chill several hours until firm enough to handle. Preheat oven to 350°F. Spray cookie sheets with non-stick coating agent. Using 1 tablespoon dough for each cookie, shape into balls and place on cookie sheets. Bake 15 to 17 minutes.

PER SERVING (1 cookie):	Calories: 60	Protein: 1gm
Carbohydrate: 9gm	Fat: 3gm	Sodium: 35mg

By using Butter Buds instead of butter in this recipe, you have saved 16 calories and 6 mg cholesterol per cookie.

Almond Cookies

 2 1/2 dozen cookies

1 cup sifted all-purpose
   flour
1/2 teaspoon baking powder
1/8 teaspoon salt
1/4 cup vegetable shortening
   or margarine
1 packet Butter Buds

1/4 cup plus 2 tablespoons
   sugar
1 egg
2 teaspoons almond
   extract
3 tablespoons sliced
   almonds

Preheat oven to 350°F. Sift together flour, baking powder, and salt. Cut in shortening. Stir in Butter Buds, sugar, egg, and almond extract to make a soft dough. Add a small amount of water if needed. Refrigerate for 15 minutes. Form into one-inch balls. Press an almond slice into the center of each ball. Arrange 2 inches apart on a non-stick cookie sheet. Bake 5 minutes, then flatten cookies with spatula to 1/4-inch thickness. Continue baking 8 to 10 minutes longer, or until lightly browned.

PER SERVING (1 cookie):	Calories: 40	Protein: trace
Carbohydrate: 6gm	Fat: 2gm	Sodium: 65mg

By using Butter Buds instead of butter in this recipe, you have saved 25 calories and 9 mg cholesterol per cookie.

Bran-Apple Cookies

 3 dozen cookies

1 2/3 cups sifted all-purpose
   flour
1 teaspoon baking soda
1/4 teaspoon nutmeg
1/4 teaspoon ground cloves
1/4 teaspoon allspice
1/4 teaspoon salt

1/2 cup diet margarine
6 packets Sweet 'N Low
1 egg
1 cup unsweetened
   applesauce
1/3 cup golden raisins
1 cup 40% bran flakes cereal

Preheat oven to 375°F. Sift dry ingredients into medium-size bowl. In separate bowl, beat margarine, Sweet 'N Low, and egg until light and fluffy. Alternately add dry ingredients and applesauce, mixing well after each addition. Stir in raisins and cereal. Drop by rounded teaspoons onto non-stick cookie sheets. Bake 15 minutes, or until golden brown.

PER SERVING (1 cookie):	Calories: 45	Protein: 1gm
Carbohydrate: 7gm	Fat: 2gm	Sodium: 70mg

Note: If you don't own non-stick cookie sheets, you can spray your cookie sheets with a non-stick coating agent.

Holiday Cookies

 2 1/2 dozen cookies

1 cup sifted all-purpose
    flour
1/4 teaspoon baking powder
1/8 teaspoon salt
1/4 cup margarine

1/4 cup sugar
1 egg
3/4 teaspoon vanilla
4 packets Sweet 'N Low

In medium-size bowl, sift together flour, baking powder, and salt. In separate bowl, cream margarine; add sugar gradually and continue creaming until light. Add egg, vanilla, and Sweet 'N Low; beat well. Thoroughly stir in dry ingredients. Refrigerate one hour.

Preheat oven to 400°F. Spray cookie sheets with non-stick coating agent. Roll dough into 3/4-inch balls. Place 2 inches apart on prepared cookie sheets; press flat with base of floured glass. Flute edges with fork. Bake 6 to 8 minutes, or until brown.

PER SERVING (1 cookie):	Calories: 35	Protein: 1gm
Carbohydrate: 5gm	Fat: 2gm	Sodium: 30mg

Note: There's no need to spray with a non-stick coating agent if you own a non-stick cookie sheet.

Fruit Nut Cookies

N·S 3 dozen cookies

1/2 cup granulated sugar
1/4 cup firmly packed light
    brown sugar
1/4 cup vegetable oil
1 egg
1/3 cup strong decaffeinated
    coffee
1 packet Butter Buds

2 teaspoons fresh lemon
    juice
1 1/2 cups sifted all-purpose
    flour
3/4 cup rolled oats
1/4 cup chopped walnuts
1/3 cup raisins

Preheat oven to 375°F. Cream sugars, oil, and egg until light and fluffy. Blend in coffee, Butter Buds, and lemon juice. Gradually add flour, mixing well after each addition. Stir in oats, nuts, and raisins. Drop by rounded teaspoons onto non-stick cookie sheets. Bake 7 to 10 minutes, or until light brown.

PER SERVING (1 cookie):	Calories: 70	Protein: 1gm
Carbohydrate: 10gm	Fat: 2gm	Sodium: 30mg

By using Butter Buds instead of butter in this recipe, you have saved 21 calories and 8 mg cholesterol per cookie.

Oatmeal Cookies 2 1/2 dozen cookies

1 cup sifted all-purpose
  flour
1/2 cup sifted whole-wheat
  flour
1/4 cup sugar
4 packets Sweet 'N Low
1 teaspoon cinnamon
1/2 teaspoon baking soda

1/4 teaspoon salt
1 egg, well beaten
1 3/4 cups rolled oats
2 packets Butter Buds,
  mixed with 1 cup water
1 cup raisins
1/4 cup low-fat milk
1 tablespoon molasses

Preheat oven to 375°F. Sift together flours, sugar, Sweet 'N Low, cinnamon, baking soda, and salt. In separate bowl, combine remaining ingredients. Add dry ingredients; mix thoroughly. Drop by rounded teaspoons onto non-stick cookie sheet. Bake 15 to 17 minutes, or until just brown.

PER SERVING (1 cookie):	Calories: 70	Protein: 2gm
Carbohydrate: 14gm	Fat: trace	Sodium: 100mg

By using Butter Buds instead of butter in this recipe, you have saved 50 calories and 15 mg cholesterol per serving.

Minnesota Harvest Bars 16 bars

1/4 cup vegetable shortening
1 packet Butter Buds, mixed
  with 2 tablespoons
  hot water
2/3 cup firmly packed light
  brown sugar
2 eggs
3/4 cup sifted all-purpose flour
1/2 teaspoon baking powder

1/2 teaspoon salt
1/2 teaspoon cinnamon
1/2 teaspoon nutmeg
1/2 teaspoon ginger
1/4 teaspoon baking soda
2/3 cup canned pumpkin
1/2 cup raisins
1/2 teaspoon vanilla

Preheat oven to 350°F. Spray 9-inch square baking pan with non-stick coating agent. In large saucepan, melt shortening over low heat. Remove from heat and stir in Butter Buds and brown sugar; beat in eggs. Add dry ingredients and mix until well blended. Stir in pumpkin, raisins, and vanilla. Pour into prepared pan and bake 25 to 30 minutes. Cool and cut into bars.

PER SERVING (1 bar):	Calories: 105	Protein: 1gm
Carbohydrate: 14gm	Fat: 4gm	Sodium: 75mg

By using Butter Buds instead of butter in this recipe, you have saved 47 calories and 18 mg cholesterol per serving.

Lemon Cake Pudding 6 servings

3 eggs, separated
2 teaspoons grated lemon peel
1/4 cup lemon juice
1 1/2 cups low-fat milk

1/4 cup sifted all-purpose
flour
8 packets Sweet 'N Low
1/8 teaspoon salt

Preheat oven to 325°F. In deep bowl, beat egg whites with electric mixer at high speed until stiff peaks form. Set aside. Add lemon peel and juice to egg yolks. Beat at medium speed until well blended. Add milk and beat at low speed 1 minute. Add flour, Sweet 'N Low, and salt; blend until smooth. Fold in egg whites by hand. Pour into 6 custard cups. Place cups in baking pan; add hot water to fill pan 1 inch. Bake 40 to 50 minutes, or until lightly browned on top. Serve warm or chilled.

PER SERVING (1/2 cup):	Calories: 90	Protein: 6gm
Carbohydrate: 9gm	Fat: 3gm	Sodium: 105mg

Super Chocolate Chip Cookies About 4 dozen cookies

1 packet Butter Buds, made
into liquid
1/4 cup vegetable oil
1 cup sugar
2 eggs
1 teaspoon vanilla
1 cup sifted all-purpose flour

1 cup sifted whole wheat flour
1 teaspoon baking soda
1/2 teaspoon salt
1 package (6 ounces)
chocolate chips
2 cups 40% bran flakes
cereal

Preheat oven to 425°F. Spray 2 cookie sheets with non-stick coating agent. In large mixing bowl, combine Butter Buds, oil, and sugar. Beat in eggs and vanilla. Mix dry ingredients; add to creamed mixture. Stir in chocolate chips and cereal. Drop by rounded teaspoons onto prepared cookie sheets. Bake 8 to 10 minutes. Remove cookies immediately to cooling racks.

PER SERVING (1 cookie):	Calories: 70	Protein: 1gm
Carbohydrate: 11gm	Fat: 3gm	Sodium: 75mg

By using Butter Buds instead of butter in this recipe, you have saved 16 calories and 6 mg cholesterol per cookie.

Note: There's no need to spray with a non-stick coating agent if you own non-stick cookie sheets.

Bananas Foster

 6 servings

1 packet Butter Buds, made
   into liquid
1 tablespoon firmly packed
   light brown sugar
4 medium (about 1 1/4
   pounds) bananas

1 tablespoon banana liqueur
2 packets Sweet 'N Low
1 tablespoon light rum
2 tablespoons brandy

Combine Butter Buds and brown sugar in skillet. Cook over medium heat until sugar dissolves. Slice bananas lengthwise and quarter. Add to skillet and sauté until tender. Gently stir in liqueur and Sweet 'N Low. Sprinkle rum and brandy over bananas; ignite before serving. Baste bananas with sauce until flames subside.

PER SERVING (1/2 cup):	Calories: 100	Protein: 1gm
Carbohydrate: 20gm	Fat: 1gm	Sodium: 150mg

By using Butter Buds instead of butter in this recipe, you have saved 125 calories and 47 mg cholesterol per serving.

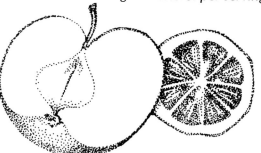

Stewed Fruit Compote

 6 servings

1/2 cup water
2 whole cinnamon sticks
1/8 teaspoon ground cloves
4 medium (about 1 pound)
   peaches, peeled, pitted
   and sliced

1 cup fresh apricots,
   pitted, or canned
   juice-packed apricot
   halves, drained
1 cup dried prunes,
   pitted
3 packets Sweet 'N Low

In medium-size saucepan, heat water, cinnamon sticks, and cloves to boiling. Add fruit; return liquid to boiling. Reduce heat to low and add Sweet 'N Low. Simmer 25 minutes, or until tender.

PER SERVING (3/4 cup):	Calories: 120	Protein: 1gm
Carbohydrate: 31gm	Fat: trace	Sodium: 5mg

Quick Crêpes Suzette 6 servings

2 packets Butter Buds, made
   into liquid
1/3 cup sugar
1 tablespoon grated orange
   peel
1 cup orange juice
2 teaspoons fresh lemon juice

12 Low-Calorie Crêpes
   (page 26)
1/4 cup apricot or peach
   brandy
1/4 cup orange-flavored
   liqueur

In a large bowl, mix together Butter Buds and sugar. Add orange peel and juices. Heat in large skillet or chafing dish. Add crêpes one at a time to mixture; turn over in sauce; fold in half and then in quarters. Move to side of pan and continue adding crêpes. Heat brandy and liqueur in separate small pan. Pour over crêpes; ignite immediately with long match. Baste crêpes with sauce in skillet until flames are extinguished. Serve immediately.

PER SERVING (2 crepes):	Calories: 200	Protein: 7gm
Carbohydrate: 34gm	Fat: 3gm	Sodium: 435mg

By using Butter Buds instead of butter in this recipe, you have saved 250 calories and 94 mg cholesterol per serving. Save 35 calories and 9 gm carbohydrate per serving by substituting 8 packets Sweet 'N Low for the sugar in this recipe.

Popcorn About 3 quarts

1 tablespoon shortening or
   vegetable oil
1/2 cup popcorn, uncooked

1/2 packet (4 teaspoons)
   Butter Buds

Measure shortening or oil into bottom of popcorn popper. Add popcorn. Cover and pop according to manufacturer's directions. When finished popping, remove from heat. Sprinkle dry Butter Buds over popcorn, tossing lightly to coat.

PER SERVING (2 cups popped):	Calories: 130	Protein: 3gm
Carbohydrate: 20gm	Fat: 5gm	Sodium: 75mg

By using Butter Buds instead of butter in this recipe, you have saved 65 calories and 25 mg cholesterol per serving.

Note: If using a heavy saucepan or skillet, heat, covered, over medium heat, and shake while corn is popping.

Low-Sodium Brownies 16 brownies

2 eggs, separated
1/4 cup plus 1 tablespoon
   granulated sugar,
   divided
1/2 cup firmly packed light
   brown sugar

1 teaspoon vanilla
1/2 cup unsweetened cocoa
1/2 cup liquid Butter Buds
1/2 cup sifted all-purpose
   flour
1/2 cup chopped walnuts

Preheat oven to 325°F. Beat yolks until light and lemon colored. Add 1/4 cup granulated sugar and brown sugar and cream until light and fluffy. Blend in vanilla, cocoa, and Butter Buds. Add flour and mix thoroughly. Stir in chopped nuts. In separate bowl, beat egg whites until firm. Add 1 tablespoon granulated sugar and beat until stiff. Fold beaten whites into batter. When completely blended, transfer batter to non-stick 8-inch square baking dish. Bake 15 minutes, or until toothpick inserted in center comes out clean.

PER SERVING (1 brownie):	Calories: 95	Protein: 2gm
Carbohydrate: 16gm	Fat: 4gm	Sodium: 65mg

By using Butter Buds instead of butter in this recipe, you have saved 47 calories and 18 mg cholesterol per brownie.

Note: If you don't own a non-stick 8-inch square baking dish, you can spray your baking dish with a non-stick coating agent.

Baked Blueberry Bread Pudding 4 servings

1 1/2 cups buttermilk
2 slices whole-wheat bread,
   broken up
2 eggs

4 packets Sweet 'N Low
1/2 teaspoon vanilla
1 cup frozen unsweetened
   blueberries

Preheat oven to 350°F. Combine all ingredients except blueberries in blender container. Cover and process on low speed about 15 seconds. Pour into 1-quart baking dish. Stir in blueberries. Bake 1 1/2 hours, or until set and browned. Serve warm or chilled.

PER SERVING (2/3 cup):	Calories: 130	Protein: 8gm
Carbohydrate: 17gm	Fat: 4gm	Sodium: 225mg

Super Chocolate Chip Cookies (page 141), Blueberry Muffins (page 32), Low-Sodium Brownies, Cranberry Nut Loaf (page 39).

Rum Baked Custard 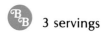 3 servings

1 packet Butter Buds
1 cup low-fat milk
1 egg, separated
1 cup (2 ounces) miniature
    marshmallows

1 teaspoon rum extract
1/8 teaspoon nutmeg

Mix Butter Buds and milk in top of double boiler. Place over simmering water. Stir until Butter Buds dissolve. Beat egg yolk and add to milk mixture. Heat, stirring constantly, until mixture thickens slightly. Remove from heat and add marshmallows, rum extract, and nutmeg. Stir until marshmallows have almost melted. Transfer to mixing bowl and let cool to room temperature.

Preheat oven to 325°F. In separate bowl, beat egg white until stiff. When marshmallow-milk mixture has cooled to room temperature, fold in egg white. Pour into 1-quart casserole sprayed with non-stick coating agent. Cover and place in pan of hot water. Bake 50 to 60 minutes, or until knife inserted in center comes out clean. Serve chilled.

PER SERVING (1/2 cup):	Calories: 135	Protein: 5gm
Carbohydrate: 21gm	Fat: 2gm	Sodium: 365mg

By using Butter Buds instead of butter in this recipe, you have saved 250 calories and 93 mg cholesterol per serving.

Prune Whip 4 servings

1 jar (5 ounces) strained
    unsweetened prunes,
    pitted
4 packets Sweet 'N Low
1 teaspoon vanilla
1 teaspoon lemon juice

1 teaspoon unflavored
    gelatin
1 tablespoon cold water
2 egg whites
4 teaspoons chopped
    walnuts

In medium-size bowl, blend prunes, Sweet 'N Low, vanilla, and lemon juice. In small saucepan, soften gelatin in cold water, placing over low heat to dissolve. In separate medium-size bowl, beat egg whites until frothy. Add dissolved gelatin and beat until stiff; fold into prune mixture. Spoon lightly into sherbet glasses. Sprinkle walnuts on top. Chill thoroughly.

PER SERVING (1/2 cup):	Calories: 95	Protein: 3gm
Carbohydrate: 18gm	Fat: 2gm	Sodium: 25mg

Mocha Spanish Cream 4 servings

1 envelope unflavored gelatin
1/4 cup cold water
2 eggs, separated
1 1/2 cups low-fat milk,
   scalded

1 teaspoon instant
   decaffeinated coffee
1/2 teaspoon vanilla
6 packets Sweet 'N Low,
   divided

In small bowl, soften gelatin in cold water. In top of double boiler, beat egg yolks; blend in milk. Cook, stirring constantly, over hot water until mixture thickens slightly. Add softened gelatin and coffee; stir until dissolved. Remove from heat. Stir in vanilla and 3 packets Sweet 'N Low. Chill until mixture is consistency of unbeaten egg whites.

In large bowl, beat egg whites with electric mixer until foamy. Add remaining Sweet 'N Low. Beat until stiff. Fold chilled custard mixture into egg whites. Pour into serving dishes. Chill until set.

PER SERVING (1/2 cup):	Calories: 105	Protein: 9gm
Carbohydrate: 7gm	Fat: 5gm	Sodium: 90mg

Rice Pudding 4 servings

1 cup low-fat milk
1 packet Butter Buds
2 eggs
2 tablespoons sugar
1 teaspoon grated lemon peel

1 teaspoon vanilla
1/2 teaspoon nutmeg
1/4 cup uncooked brown
   rice
1/4 cup raisins

Preheat oven to 325°F. Heat milk in saucepan. Add Butter Buds and stir until dissolved. Heat until mixture simmers. Remove from heat. In separate bowl, beat eggs until frothy. Add sugar, lemon peel, vanilla, and nutmeg. Add to milk mixture. Add rice and raisins. Mix well. Pour into 1-quart baking dish. Sprinkle with additional nutmeg. Bake for 30 minutes, or until knife inserted near center comes out clean.

PER SERVING (1/2 cup):	Calories: 170	Protein: 6gm
Carbohydrate: 30gm	Fat: 3gm	Sodium: 385mg

By using Butter Buds instead of butter in this recipe, you have saved 188 calories and 70 mg cholesterol per serving. You can also substitute 3 packets Sweet 'N Low for the sugar in this recipe and save 20 calories and 6 gm carbohydrate per serving.

Banana Fluff

 4 servings

1 envelope unflavored gelatin
1 packet Butter Buds
1/4 cup sugar
1 1/4 cups low-fat milk
1 teaspoon vanilla

1 egg, separated
2 small ripe bananas (7 ounces peeled), thinly sliced
2 teaspoons lemon juice

Combine gelatin, Butter Buds, sugar, and milk in top of double boiler. Place over simmering water. Stir until Butter Buds dissolve. Add vanilla and beaten egg yolk. Heat until mixture thickens slightly, stirring constantly. Remove from heat; cool until mixture thickens further. Stir in bananas and lemon juice. Beat egg white until stiff and fold into gelatin mixture. Pour into individual dessert dishes. Chill.

PER SERVING (1/2 cup):	Calories: 150	Protein: 6gm
Carbohydrate: 27gm	Fat: 2gm	Sodium: 280mg

By using Butter Buds instead of butter in this recipe, you have saved 188 calories and 70 mg cholesterol per serving.

Note: You'll save 40 calories and 10 gm carbohydrate per serving by substituting 6 packets Sweet 'N Low for the sugar in this recipe.

Baked Apples

 4 servings

2 tablespoons sugar
1 packet Butter Buds
1/2 teaspoon cinnamon

1/8 teaspoon nutmeg
4 baking apples, cored
1/4 cup raisins

Preheat oven to 350°F. Combine sugar, Butter Buds, cinnamon, and nutmeg. Sprinkle in apple cavity. Add 1 tablespoon raisins to each apple. Place apples in baking dish and bake 30 to 40 minutes, or until soft.

PER SERVING (1 apple):	Calories: 165	Protein: trace
Carbohydrate: 35gm	Fat: 1gm	Sodium: 225mg

By using Butter Buds instead of butter in this recipe, you have saved 188 calories and 70 mg cholesterol per serving. You can also substitute 3 packets Sweet 'N Low for the sugar in this recipe and save 20 calories per serving.

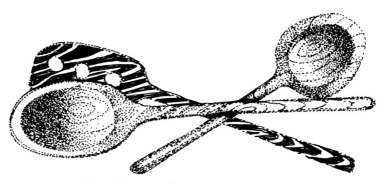

Steamed Chocolate Pudding

 6 servings

1 egg, separated	2 teaspoons baking powder
3/4 cup sugar, divided	3/4 cup low-fat milk
2 teaspoons vanilla	1 cup sifted all-purpose
1/2 teaspoon cinnamon	flour
1/4 teaspoon salt	1 packet Butter Buds
1/2 cup unsweetened cocoa	

Beat egg yolk with electric mixer until light, about 2 minutes. Add 1/2 cup sugar, vanilla, cinnamon, and salt. Beat until light and fluffy, about 2 minutes. Combine cocoa and baking powder; add to creamed mixture on low speed. Gradually blend in milk. Add flour, 1/4 cup at a time, beating constantly. When all flour has been mixed in, add Butter Buds and beat on medium speed for 12 to 15 seconds. Do not overmix. In separate bowl, beat egg white until soft peaks form. Gradually add remaining 1/4 cup sugar, beating until stiff. Fold beaten egg white into batter until completely blended (use rubber scraper for best results). Spray 1-quart covered baking dish with non-stick coating agent. Pour batter into dish and cover tightly. Place on rack in large kettle or dutch oven. Add boiling water to come halfway up sides of dish. Cover kettle and steam pudding for about 1 hour, or until toothpick inserted in center comes out clean. Unmold immediately and serve with low-calorie whipped topping, if desired. Serve warm.

PER SERVING (1/2 cup):	Calories: 210	Protein: 5gm
Carbohydrate: 44gm	Fat: 2gm	Sodium: 210mg

By using Butter Buds instead of butter in this recipe, you have saved 125 calories and 47 mg cholesterol per serving.

Note: There's no need to spray with a non-stick coating agent if you own a non-stick baking dish.

Trim Slim Custard

 2 servings

2 eggs
2 packets Sweet 'N Low
1 teaspoon vanilla

1 1/2 cups skim milk, scalded
Nutmeg

Preheat oven to 350°F. In medium-size bowl, beat eggs slightly. Add Sweet 'N Low and vanilla; slowly stir in milk. Pour into two 1-cup custard cups; set in shallow pan filled with 1 inch of hot water. Sprinkle with nutmeg. Bake 30 minutes, or until knife inserted in center comes out clean.

PER SERVING (3/4 cup):	Calories: 150	Protein: 13gm
Carbohydrate: 10gm	Fat: 6gm	Sodium: 155mg

Poached Pears with Blueberry Sauce

 8 servings

8 medium-size (about 2 1/2 pounds) fresh pears
1 packet Butter Buds
1 cup water
3 tablespoons lemon juice

4 packets Sweet 'N Low
2 cups fresh or frozen unsweetened blueberries
1/4 cup port wine

Preheat oven to 350°F. Peel pears, leaving stems intact; do not core. Arrange with stems up in 3-quart casserole; set aside. Combine Butter Buds, water, lemon juice, and Sweet 'N Low; mix well. Pour over pears. Bake, covered, 45 minutes, or until pears are tender. Drain and chill, about 45 minutes.

In blender container, process blueberries and wine, covered, on low several seconds, or until well blended. Place pears in shallow dish and pour blueberry sauce over top. Refrigerate, turning pears occasionally to coat well. Serve in dessert dishes topped with plain low-fat yogurt, if desired.

PER SERVING (1 pear):	Calories: 140	Protein: 1gm
Carbohydrate: 30gm	Fat: trace	Sodium: 115mg

By using Butter Buds instead of butter in this recipe, you have saved 94 calories and 35 mg cholesterol per serving.

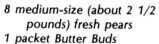

Index

154

Recipes Grouped by Products